SIMPLY KIXTART

To Kixtart with love

Richard Edwards

CONTENTS

What, you want to drop out??

This is an e-book, not a classroom!

My first experience of a student wanting to drop out of a college class was based on a heated conversation between the professor and the student. I'm not quite certain why the student felt the way she did considering the professor was an excellent, well known poet.

But for some reason only known to her, she didn't take much liking to him and she wasn't in his class past that point.

Which brings me to my real point that I want to make in your behalf. I don't have to be liked by you. Nor do you have to return the favor. The bottom line here is you are investing the use of your time, effort and money into this book because it is going to gratify your interest of wanting to learn a programming language.

One that, in return is going to make you look smarter on paper, increase your wages and otherwise help you become the superman or superwoman.

Well, I can't promise that. At least, not all of that.

You are paying me to share with you my 30 years-worth of time in front of a computer screen in hopes some of that genie stuff will wear off on you. I can't promise that either. Yes, I am well familiar with the fact that this is the chapter where you decide to purchase this e-book. But, I don't want to motivate you if you're just looking for page after page of code.

You can get that from the internet for free. Instead, I'm taking a more relaxed approach and hope you will appreciate the fact that I know learning a computer language is more than knowing what is needed to code with it.

You must sell yourself and your skills to others. After all, if you can't do that, I don't care how popular the language is, it is not helping you land a job or the right to respectful wages.

Otherwise, nothing changes in your life no matter how passionate you are about becoming a freelance programmer or IT consultant. Still want to close the introduction to this book and walk away?

Great!

I don't have to worry about you being my competition the next time I go in for an interview.

What the heck is Kixtart?

Okay, I need to quit with the wise cracks. Somebody is going to get peeved. Kixtart was a brilliant, very challenging VBScript style code that – as far as I'm concerned – was the forerunner for PowerShell. Unfortunately, it has been demoted to a careware language. RIP Kixtart.

So, why use a careware language?

Because it is interesting in the way it appears – only appears -- to work just like VBScript.

And believe me, sometimes the old is just as good as the new.

How to install this

First, on your desktop, create a folder then use this link and at the very top of the page, download the very top build as shown below:

KiXtart 2010 4.60 (2nd of October 2007) KiX2010_460.zip (876kB)
Once it is downloaded go to your downloads and find the zip file. Unzip the contents to the folder you just created. When done, go to your Kixtart folder and you should see and another folder: KiX2010.467.
Open this up and this is what you should see:

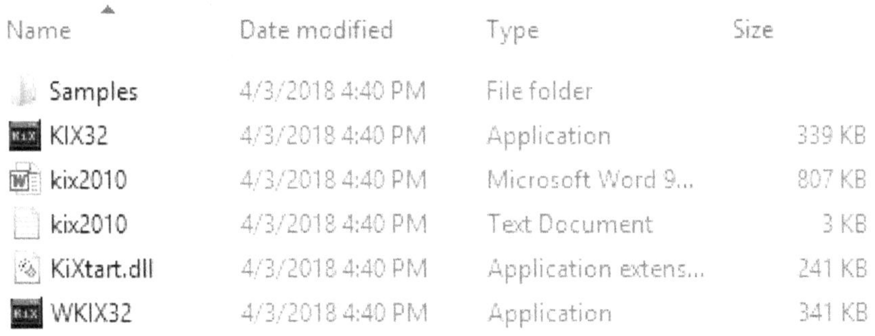

Name	Date modified	Type	Size
Samples	4/3/2018 4:40 PM	File folder	
KIX32	4/3/2018 4:40 PM	Application	339 KB
kix2010	4/3/2018 4:40 PM	Microsoft Word 9...	807 KB
kix2010	4/3/2018 4:40 PM	Text Document	3 KB
KiXtart.dll	4/3/2018 4:40 PM	Application extens...	241 KB
WKIX32	4/3/2018 4:40 PM	Application	341 KB

Open a new instance of notepad and type in:
Messagebox("Hello from Kixtart", "Kixtart")
Don't cut and paste. The quotes in this book cause issues.
Once you've typed in the Messagebox stuff, type in "Starter.kix" and save the file in the KiX2010.467 folder.
Once done, click on the new file and select Open With and then choose a default program. At this point, another window will open making some suggestions, click on more options and then scroll down to the bottom of the page it will say, look for other options on this PC.
After you've selected that option, go to desktop\Kixtart\KiX2010.467 Folder.

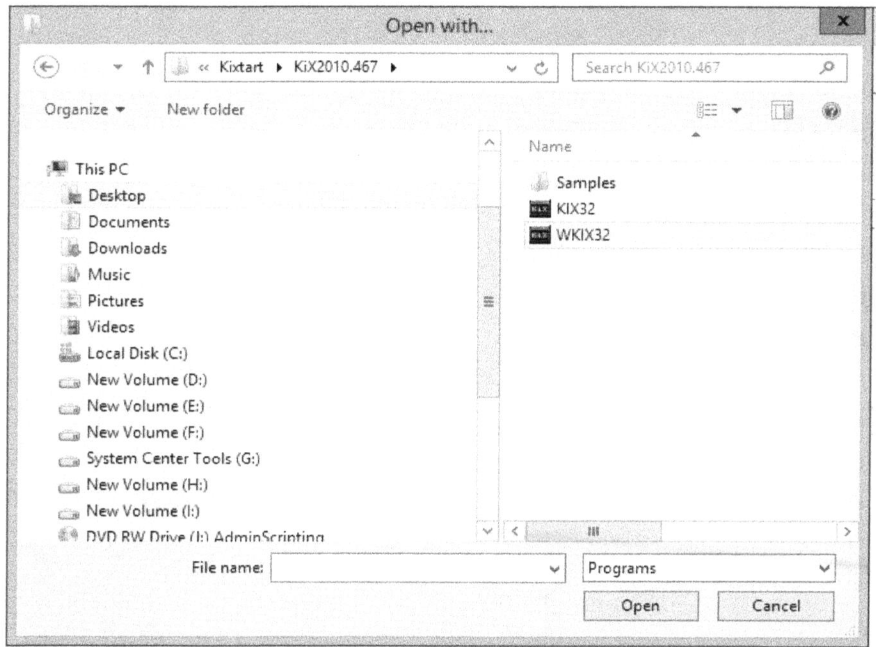

Move your mouse pointer over WKIX32 and double click on it. The Dialog box will go away, and your Starter will now have an icon looking like this:

When you run it, you should see the following:

Name	Date modified	Type	Size
Samples	4/3/2018 4:40 PM	File folder	
KIX32	4/3/2018 4:40 PM	Application	339 KB
kix2010	4/3/2018 4:40 PM	Microsoft Word 9...	807 KB
kix2010	4/3/2018 4:40 PM	Text Document	3 KB
KiXtart.dll	4/3/2018 4:40 PM	Application extens...	241 KB
Starter	4/3/2018 9:03 PM	KIX File	1 KB
WKIX32	4/3/2018 4:40 PM	Application	341 KB

And we're well on our way. (snuck that one in, didn't I?)
There's a song with the same a similar line and it made millions. Doubt that I using the same will have a similar effect on my life. I'm also at the other end of the life cycle spectrum. And I can tell you right now, the times that I got hired for a job in IT, was because I gave them a story that went like this:
Before you met me, you didn't realize how much value and important I am to you and your team's desire to accomplishing the task at hand. Now that you've met me, you know I am the asset you were looking for and have no choice but to hire me on the spot.
The name of the game here is **the art of selling**. One I pretty much wrote back in the '80s.
Okay, so as you have just discovered, a msgbox in the Kixtart world is a MessageBox and you must add a title it.

But you can also use:

```
$ws= CreateObject("Wscript.Shell")
$ws.Popup(your name in quotes)
```

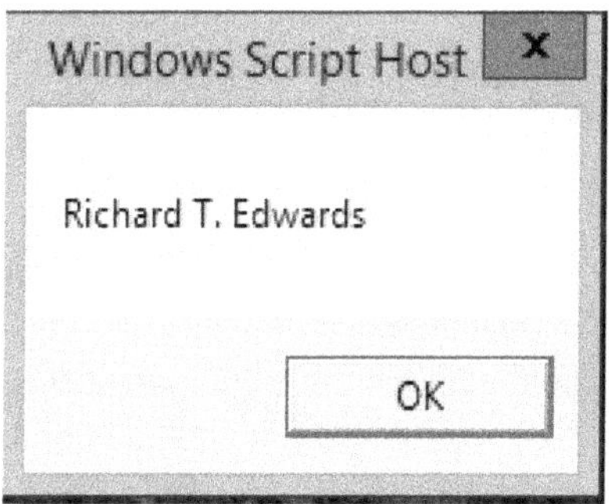

Which will also create a popup Messagebox to display information your end user can interact with.

There was some chatter on the Internet that you could use InputBox, but I tried it and I just couldn't get it to work. Notice that you use $ on everything you create as variables. No Dim statements or Set statements just a $ sign.

Getting Ready to Rumble

Let's start priming the pump

Creating a Notepad shortcut

Again, right click inside the folder area. Go down to where you see new. Once selected another menu will appear as it did when you created a new folder and just below it, you will see the word Shortcut.

A window will appear and ask you for the location and name of the file. Click browse. Go to your windows drive and click on Windows. Once you are in that directory, look for Notepad and click on it and then click okay. The window will return with the location of the file – which, you could have just copy and pasted this into the textbox:

C:\Windows\notepad.exe

Click next and then click Finish. You now have a shortcut that is easier to use then having to go to start, run and type in Notepad.

12 keys to the kingdom

The blueprint to all COM related programs

1. The creation of an object
2. The use of a property to get\$a value
3. The use of a function that does or does not accept parameters and may or may not return a value. Functions are also called methods.
4. The use of an event that occurs and you write code to respond to it.
5. The use of enumerators
6. The use of conditional Loops
7. The use of conditional branches
8. The use of error trapping
9. Data Conversions
10. Constants
11. Declarations
12. Reg Expressions

You know, instead of talking about all of this – which usually occupies about 20 pages, let's do something different.

Welcome To WMI

Full WMI ASYNC EXAMPLE

```
Private Sub sink_OnObjectReady($objWbemObject, $objWbemAsyncContext)
   For Each prop in $objWbemObject.Properties_
      $V = $V + $prop.Name & " " & GetValue($prop.Name, $objWbemObject) &
vbCrLf
   Next
   MsgBox ($v)
End Sub
Private Sub sink_OnCompleted($iHResult, $objWbemErrorObject,
$objWbemAsyncContext)
   $w = 1
End Sub
$w = 0
$ns = "root\Cimv2"
$Classname = "Win32_BIOS"
$locator = CreateObject("WbemScripting.SWbemLocator")
$svc = $locator.ConnectServer(".", ns)
$svc.Security_.AuthenticationLevel = 6
$svc.Security_.ImpersonationLevel = 3
$sink = WScript.CreateObject("WBemScripting.SWbemSink", "SINK_")
Call $svc.ExecQueryAsync(sink, "Select * From " & Classname)
Do While $w = 0
  WScript.Sleep(500)
Loop
```

FULL SYNC EXAMLE

```
On Error Resume Next
Dim ns
Dim Classname

$ns = "root\Cimv2"
$Classname = "Win32_BIOS"

$locator = CreateObject("WbemScripting.SWbemLocator")
$svc = $locator.ConnectServer(".", ns)
$svc.Security_.AuthenticationLevel=6")
$svc.Security_.ImpersonationLevel=3")
$objs = $svc.ExecQuery("Select * From " & classname)
For Each $obj in $objs
   For Each $prop in $obj.Properties_
            $v=$v + $prop.Name & " " & getValue($prop.Name, $obj) & vbcrlf
   Next
Next
MessageBox($v)
```

And that pretty much covers what the code is doing. But this is common code. Meaning,
In VBScript, it would be written this way:

```
Ser l = CreateObject("WbemScripting.SWbemLocator")
Set svc = l.ConnectServer(".", "root\cimv2")
svc.Security_.AuthenticationLevel = 6
svc.Security_.ImpersonationLevel = 3
Set objs = $svc.InstancesOf("Win32_Process")

For Each obj in objs
     For Each prop in obj.Properties_

     Next
Next
```

In Kixtart:

```
$l = new-object -com WbemScripting.SWbemLocator
$svc = $l.ConnectServer(".", "root\cimv2")
$svc.Security_.AuthenticationLevel = 6
$svc.Security_.ImpersonationLevel = 3
$objs = $svc.InstancesOf("Win32_Process")

foreach($obj in $objs)
{
    foreach($prop in $obj.Properties_)
    {
    }
}
```

Okay, so now what?
Well., we could look at the GetValue function that we originally used. After all, it is one of the best parsing routines and it does get the job done.
Instead, it will be on the following page for you to learn from as it pretty much does almost everything you would want to do to get what you want from a string you want to parse.

Working with text files

The next couple of pages are devoted to text files. The format is in csv. But you can change it and the .csv extension to .txt and then change the delimiter:

This is for csv:	$tempstr + “,”
This is for tab:	$tempstr + vbtab
This is for semi-colon:	$tempstr + “;”
This is for colon:	$tempstr + “:”
This is for tilde:	$tempstr + “~”
This is for Exclamation:	$tempstr + “!”

Using ADO to create a CSV file

```
$cn = CreateObject("ADODB.Connection")
$cmd = CreateObject("ADODB.Command")
$rs = CreateObject("ADODB.Recordset")

$cn.ConnectionString = "Provider=Microsoft.Jet.OLEDB.4.0;Data
Source=C:\NWIND.MDB;"
```

```
$cn.Open()

$rs.ActiveConnection = $cn
$rs.LockType = 3
$rs.CursorLocation = 3
$rs.Source = "Select * from [Products]"
$rs.Open()

$tempstr=""

$ws = CreateObject("WScript.Shell")
$fso = CreateObject("Scripting.FileSystemObject")
$txtstream = $fso.OpenTextFile("C:\Products.csv", 2, true, -2)
$count = $rs.Fields.Count -1
for $x = 0 To $count
            If  $tempstr <> ""
               $tempstr = $tempstr  + ","
   EndIf
   $tempstr + $tempstr + $rs.Fields($x).Name
Next
$txtstream.WriteLine($tempstr)
$tempstr = ""


$rs.MoveLast()
$rs.MoveFirst()
while($rs.eof = false)
            for $x = 0 To $count
                        If  $tempstr <> ""
                                    $tempstr = $tempstr  + ","
                        EndIf
            $tempstr + $tempstr + chr(34) + $rs.Fields($x).Value + chr(34)
            Next
            $txtstream.WriteLine($tempstr)
            $tempstr = ""
    $rs.MoveNext()
Loop
$txtstream.close
```

Using DAO to CREATE a CSV file

```
$dbEngine = CreateObject("DAO.DBEngine.36")
$db = $dbEngine.OpenDatabase("C:\Nwind.mdb")
$rs = $db.OpenRecordset("Products")

$tempstr=""

$ws = CreateObject("WScript.Shell")
$fso = CreateObject("Scripting.FileSystemObject")
$txtstream = $fso.OpenTextFile("C:\Products.csv", 2, true, -2)
$count = $rs.Fields.Count -1
for $x = 0 To $count
            If  $tempstr <> ""
               $tempstr = $tempstr  + ","
   EndIf
   $tempstr + $tempstr + $rs.Fields($x).Name
Next
$txtstream.WriteLine($tempstr)
$tempstr = ""

$rs.MoveLast()
$rs.MoveFirst()
while($rs.eof = false)
            for $x = 0 To $count
                        If  $tempstr <> ""
                                    $tempstr = $tempstr  + ","
                        EndIf
            $tempstr + $tempstr + chr(34) + $rs.Fields($x).Value + chr(34)
            Next
            $txtstream.WriteLine($tempstr)
            $tempstr = ""
   $rs.MoveNext()
Loop
$txtstream.close
```

Using WMI to create a CSV file

Here's what the core code looks like:

```
$crlf = Chr(13) + Chr(10)

$tempstr
$Name
$Value
$v

$l = CreateObject("WbemScripting.SWbemLocator")
$svc = $l.ConnectServer(".", "root\cimv2")
$svc.Security_.AuthenticationLevel = 6
$svc.Security_.ImpersonationLevel = 3
$objs = $svc.InstancesOf("Win32_Process")

$ws = CreateObject("WScript.Shell")
$fso = CreateObject("Scripting.FileSystemObject")
$v=0

$txtstream = $fso.OpenTextFile($ws.CurrentDirectory + "\Win32_Process.csv", 2,
True, -2)
 For Each $obj in $objs
    If v = 0 then
      For Each $prop in $obj.Properties_
         If $strName <> ""
            $strName = $strName + ","
         Endif
         $strName = $strName + $prop.Name
      Next
      $txtstream.WriteLine($strName)
      $strName = ""
      v=1
    Endif
    For Each $prop in $obj.Properties_
```

```
        If $strValue <> ""
          $strValue = $strValue + ","
        Endif
            $strValue = $strValue + chr(34) + GetValue($prop.Name, $obj) + chr(34)
    Next
    $txtstream.WriteLine($strValue)
    $strValue = ""
Next
$txtstream.Close

function GetValue($Name, $obj)

  $tempstr = $obj.GetObjectText_;
  $pname = $Name + " = "
  $pos = InStr($tempstr, $pname)
  If($pos > 0)
     $pos = $pos + Len($pname)
     $l = Len($tempstr)
     $l = $l - $pos
     $tempstr = SUBSTR($tempstr, $pos, $l)
     $p = instr($tempstr, ";")
     $tempstr = SUBSTR($tempstr, 1, $p-1)
     $tempstr = REPLACE($tempstr,"{", "")
     $tempstr = REPLACE($tempstr,"}", "")
     $tempstr = REPLACE($tempstr, chr(34), "")
     if($obj.Properties_.Item($Name).CIMType = 101)
  if(Len($tempstr) > 12)
    $tempstr = substr($tempstr, 5,2) + "/" + substr($tempstr, 7,2) + "/" +
substr($tempstr, 1,4) + " " + substr($tempstr, 9,2) + ":" + substr($tempstr, 11,2) +
":" + substr($tempstr, 13,2)
  EndIf
     EndIf
     $GetValue = $tempstr
  Else
     $GetValue = ""
  EndIf

EndFunction
```

That looks very intimidating, so, let's get rid of all the fluff.

```
$crlf = Chr(13) + Chr(10)

$l = CreateObject("WbemScripting.SWbemLocator")
$svc = $l.ConnectServer(".", "root\cimv2")
$svc.Security_.AuthenticationLevel = 6
$svc.Security_.ImpersonationLevel = 3
$objs = $svc.InstancesOf("Win32_Process")

For Each $obj in $objs
    For Each $prop in $obj.Properties_

    Next
Next
```

Looks a lot tamer, doesn't it? So, what are we looking at?

First, the code created a Carriage Return (the cr) and line feed (the lf) – using the Chr(13) and (+) Chr(10).

Then there was an object created that enables the program to use around 20,000 different classes that are on each computer. These classes are on your machine and are accessible through WMI or Windows Management Instrumentation.

In this case, the way to get to them is through WbemScripting.SWbemLocator. And by the way, Wbem means Web Based Enterprise Management.

Once the object is created, SWbemServices = the $svc is used to bind to a local connection and the namespace we want to go to is "root\CimV2".

The $l.ConnectServer can also connect to a remote machine and UserName and Password can be added to the connection. But on a local connection they aren't required and if you did try to use them collecting locally, you would get an error.

Because we're using COM and going through DCOM, the program is setting some security properties. AuthenticationLevel and ImpersonationLevel are given the values need to using DCOM and – if this is a cold connection, it could take up to 40 seconds before the hand shaking is done and you are connected – even to the local machine.

Next, there is the use of 4 synchronous and 4 asynchronous functions that can be called from the WbemServices class. Get, InstancesOf, ExecNotificationQuery and

ExecQuery. The Async versions are GetAsync, InstancesOfAsync, ExecNotificationQueryAsync and ExecQueryAsync.

In this case, the code is using InstancesOf and is passing in Win32_Process.

This call with return a collection of objects, hence $objs.

There are a variety of ways this collection can be enumerated through; the program is using the For Each $obj in $objs for the objects or rows and he For Each $prop in $obj.Properties_ to enumerate through the columns or properties collection.

Connection Strings

No matter how good you get at creating database related objects, no matter how much you know about making them work interactively, true is, you aren't going to do a thing without a solid knowledge of connection strings and SQL Queries.
What, exactly, is a connection string?
It is a $of properties vital to a connection with a specific kind of database engine in mind that are placed together as a single string.
While that sounds too simple to be almost laughable, you might want to go here. That might make the simple serious.

Some typical Connection Strings

Provider=Microsoft.Jet.OLEDB.3.51;
Data Source: C:\Program Files (x86)\Microsoft Visual Studio\VB98\NWind.mdb;

Provider=Microsoft.Jet.OLEDB.4.0;
Data Source: C:\Program Files (x86)\Microsoft Visual Studio\VB98\NWind.mdb;

Provider= Microsoft.ACE.OLEDB.10.0;
Data Source: C:\NWind.accdb;

Provider= Microsoft.ACE.OLEDB.12.0;
Data Source: C:\NWind.accdb;

Provider= Microsoft.ACE.OLEDB.15.0;
Data Source: C:\NWind.accdb;

Provider= Microsoft.ACE.OLEDB.16.0;
Data Source: C:\NWind.accdb;

Simply ADO

ADO is an acronym for Active-X Data Objects. In Kixtart, you can use it to connect to both the 32 bit and 64-bit versions of Providers, Drivers and ISAMS
The reason why ADO came about in the first place was because DAO relied a lot on disk drives to do most of the work and disk drives were extremely slow.
It is also what was used to build the .Net ODBC, OLEDB, Oracle Client and SQL Client components. So, everything you do in ADO can be applied to the various .Net world as well. Therefore, if you learn ADO, the others are self-explanatory and a walk in the park.
This toolkit includes:

- ADODB.Connection
- ADODB.Command
- ADODB.RecordSet

While I love working with SQL Server, I use it in its simplest of terms. I create a connection string cnstr and then a strQuery as my SQL query string.

Here' how these combinations have been worked with in the past:

- Connection, Command and Recordset
- Connection and Recordset
- Command and Recordset
- Recordset

Most of my experiences deal with these four conventions although I have used the ADODB.STREAM with XML and ADSI.
Below are what you will see when these are combined:

Connection, Command and Recordset

```
$cn = CreateObject("Adodb.Connection")
$cmd = CreateObject("Adodb.Command")
$rs = CreateObject("Adodb.Recordset")
$cn.ConnectionString = cnstr
Call $cn.Open()

$cmd.ActiveConnection = cn
$cmd.CommandType = 1
$cmd.CommandText = strQuery
$rs = $cmd.Execute()
```

Okay so, what is this used for? This code example is used to produce a forward only recordset. It is fast. But you can't use it for adding additional rows or perform edits and updates.

If you're wanting a more robust coding scenario, you'll want to use the connection and Recordset combination or just the recordset.

However, the combination of all three can produce a Recordset that can be used for adding records and editing and updating columns.

```
$cn = CreateObject("Adodb.Connection")
$cmd = CreateObject("Adodb.Command")
$rs = CreateObject("Adodb.Recordset")
$cn.ConnectionString = $cnstr
Call $cn.Open()
$cmd.ActiveConnection = cn
$cmd.CommandType = 1
$cmd.CommandText = strQuery
$cmd.Execute()
$rs.ActiveConnection = cn
$rs.Cursorlocation = 3
$rs.Locktype = 3
Call $rs.Open(cmd)
   For Each $obj in $objs
     $rs.AddNew()
     For Each $prop in $obj.Properties_
        $rs.fields($prop.Name).Value = GetValue($prop.Name, $obj)
     Next
$rs.Update
```

Connection and Recordset

```
$cmd = CreateObject("Adodb.Command")
$rs = CreateObject("Adodb.Recordset")
$cmd.ActiveConnection = cnstr
$cmd.CommandType = 1
$cmd.CommandText = strQuery
$cmd.Execute()
$rs.Cursorlocation = 3
$rs.Locktype = 3
$rs.Open(cmd)
```

Command and Recordset

```
$cmd = CreateObject("Adodb.Command")
$rs = CreateObject("Adodb.Recordset")
$cmd.ActiveConnection = cnstr
$cmd.CommandType = 1
$cmd.CommandText = strQuery
$rs = $cmd.Execute()
Or
Call $cmd.Execute()
$rs.Cursorlocation = 3
$rs.Locktype = 3
$rs.Open(cmd)
For Each $obj in $objs
            $rs.AddNew()
            For Each $prop in $obj.Properties_
         $rs.fields($prop.Name).Value = GetValue($prop.Name, $obj)
            Next
            $rs.Update()
Next
```

Recordset

```
  $rs = CreateObject("Adodb.Recordset")
```

```
$rs.ActiveConnection = cnstr
$rs.Cursorlocation = 3
$rs.Locktype = 3
$rs.Source = strQuery
$rs.Open()
```

ISAMS

Did you know you can use a wide variety of text files as databases?

It's true, in fact, if you have a table inside a webpage, using the right ISAM or ODBC Driver, you can connect to it and glean from it the table information and convert it into a different type of database format.

In plain English, it is a text file. The idea was to take a folder and call it a database and then take a file and call it a table. Like the way JSOM works.

One of the biggest issues – and one that brought smiles to our technical support faces – was to explain, politely to our customers that the reason why they were getting an error when they tried to create a database was the fact that the folder already existed.

Every text file you create will have delimiter. Otherwise, placing information into a text file would be just another text file and you couldn't reuse the information because there would be nothing a program – including ours – could use to separate one field from another.

These are all various files we're going to be covering, so they really don't change that much. But they are used quite often as data storage and data files.

Of course, CSV or coma delimited is just one of dozens of $possibilities. And all of these are easy to code. You enumerate through names and values and then add the delimiter of choice to separate the fields.

Problem is, it doesn't work. At least, not yet. It will soon. In fact, after I get done with it, you are going to become a master of Delimited files.

ISAMS USED WITH MICROSFT JET OLEDB 3.51

ISAM Engine	Is the Folder Path The Database	Is the File Name The Database	Are Tables Internal

dBase 5.0	Yes	No	No
dBase III	Yes	No	No
dBase IV	Yes	No	No
Excel 3.0	No	Yes	Yes
Excel 4.0	No	Yes	Yes
Excel 5.0	No	Yes	Yes
Excel 6.0	No	Yes	Yes
FoxPro 2.0	Yes	No	No
FoxPro 2.5	Yes	No	No
FoxPro 2.6	Yes	No	No
FoxPro 3.0	Yes	No	No
HTML Export	No	Yes	Yes
HTML Import	No	Yes	Yes
Jet 2.x	No	Yes	Yes
Lotus WK1	Yes	No	No
Lotus WK3	Yes	No	No
Lotus WK4	Yes	No	No
Paradox 3.X	Yes	No	No
Paradox 4.X	Yes	No	No
Paradox 5.X	Yes	No	No
Text	No	No	No

Provider=Microsoft.Jet.OLEDB.3.51;

Data Source: C:\ISAMS;

Extended Properties: "dBaseIII; hdr=yes;";

What this table is telling you

Database is the path.

The File Name is the database

The file itself contains tables

Suppose, for example, you wanted to open a dBase III database. Your Data Source would be the folder location where the file resides. The Query would be based on the filename: "Select * From [myDbase.dbf]"

If you wanted to open an HTML File. Your Data Source would be the Full path to where the file resides: C:\HTML\myhtml.html.

The Query would be bases on the filename: "Select * From [Table1]"

If you wanted to open a text file. Your Data Source would be the folder location where the file resides. The Query would be based on the filename: "Select * From [Myfile.txt]"

ISAMS USED WITH Microsoft.Jet.OLEDB.4.0;

ISAM Engine	Is the Folder Path The Database	Is the File Name The Database	Are Tables Internal
dBase 5.0	Yes	No	No
dBase III	Yes	No	No
dBase IV	Yes	No	No
Excel 3.0	No	Yes	Yes
Excel 4.0	No	Yes	Yes
Excel 5.0	No	Yes	Yes
Excel 8.0	No	Yes	Yes
HTML Export	No	Yes	Yes
HTML Import	No	Yes	Yes
Jet 2.x	No	Yes	Yes
Lotus WJ2	Yes	No	No
Lotus WJ3	Yes	No	No
Lotus WK1	Yes	No	No

Lotus WK3	Yes	No	No
Lotus WK4	Yes	No	No
Paradox 3.X	Yes	No	No
Paradox 4.X	Yes	No	No
Paradox 5.X	Yes	No	No
Text	No	No	No

Provider=Microsoft.Jet.OLEDB.4.0;

Data Source: C:\Program Files (x86)\Microsoft Visual Studio\VB98\NWind.mdb;

Data Source: C:\ISAMS;

Extended Properties: "dBaseIII; hdr=yes;";

What this table is telling you

Database is the path.

The File Name is the database

The file itself contains tables

Suppose, for example, you wanted to open a dBase III database. Your Data Source would be the folder location where the file resides. The Query would be based on the filename: "Select * From [myDbase.dbf]"

If you wanted to open an HTML File. Your Data Source would be the Full path to where the file resides: C:\HTML\myhtml.html.

The Query would be bases on the filename: "Select * From [Table1]"

If you wanted to open a text file. Your Data Source would be the folder location where the file resides. The Query would be based on the filename: "Select * From [Myfile.txt]"

Using ADOX to create an Access Database

While ADOX can create a Database and a Table, we use an ADODB Recordset to populate it. Because of that reason I don't expect to find out the Value of an ADODB.Recordset is going the way of DAO.

But who knows?

ADOX was originally designed to make Access Databases more secure and to provide both a Database creation and connection capability through its ADOX.Catalog.

But it became more popular with developers and programmers because it was easy to use, provided a more ADO look and feel and didn't limit the Data Types to just those used by DAO. So, it was faster, flexible and more robust.

Until, that is, SSD drives and enhanced hard drives were created making DAO just as fast as ADO.

Anyway, I've posted the code below that was used to create the Database and Table. Code was also added to populate the Database using an ADODB.Recordset.

Need to explain the additional try catch on this routine. Win32_Service works perfectly fine. But someone decided on their service entry to add two additional fields. Without the try catch, Kixtart would throw an exception and I didn't want to have it do that.

```
$oCat = CreateObject("ADOX.Catalog")
```

```
$oTable = CreateObject("ADOX.Table")

$ocat.Create("Provider=Microsoft.Jet.OleDb.4.0;Data
Source=C:\ADOXDatabase.mdb")
$oTable.Name = "Processes"
$oTable.ParentCatalog = $oCat
$Locale = "MS_0409"
$Authentication = 6
$Impersonation = 3
$svc = GetObject("winmgmts:[locale=MS-409]\\.\root\cimv2")
$svc.Security_.AuthenticationLevel = 6
$svc.Security_.ImpersonationLevel=  3
$objs = $svc.InstancesOf("Win32_Process")
foreach($obj in $objs)
{
   foreach($prop in $obj.Properties_)
   {
      $col = new-object -com ADOX.Column
      $col.Name = $prop.Name
      $col.Type = 203
      $oTable.Columns.Append($Col)
   }
   break
}
$oCat.Tables.Append($oTable)
$oTable = $null
$oCat = $null

$rs = new-object -com ADODB.Recordset
$rs.LockType = 3
$rs.CursorLocation = 3
$rs.Open("Select * from Services", "Provider=Microsoft.Jet.OleDb.4.0;Data
Source=C:\ADOXDatabase.mdb")

foreach($obj in $objs)
{
   $rs.AddNew()
   foreach($prop in $obj.Properties_)
   {
      try
```

```
    {
        $Name = $prop.Name
        $Value = GetValue $prop.Name $obj
        $rs.Fields.Item($Name).Value = $Value
    }
    catch
    {
    }
  }
  $rs.Update()
}
$rs.Close()
```

DAO the Godfather of Data Access

When I came to work for Microsoft in 1996, the only way to communicate with any database that was currently being used with Microsoft Windows Products was Data Access Object or DAO for short.

DAO could connect to local or remote machines and was – still is – one of the most powerful and impressive means through which one could work with data.

The reason why Active-X Data Objects(ADO) was created because it used memory instead of physical drive space DAO was well known for using. Making it slower with respect to drive verses memory.

Well, today, the speed of USB hard drives and SSD Drives makes the speed differences between memory and physical drives a mute-point.

But there was also another reason why DAO was put on the back burner.

SQL Server.

It isn't hard to imagine why. DAO connecting to a remote machine where the database was located works much like SQL Server clients can connect to a remote version of SQL Server. But DAO wasn't and still isn't limited to just SQL Server.

It can connect to all different kinds of databases such as Indexed Sequential Access Method or ISAM and Open Database Connectivity (ODBC) drivers can be used as well.

While it is true that ADO can do the same, A lot of what ADO uses and, for certain, what the .Net Framework uses has been built on top of DAO and ODBC advanced programmer's interfaces (APIs). Which is why specific types of Namespaces: ADO, ODBC, OLEDB, and SQL Client exists as separate ways to connect to different database types.

A Normal Connection using DAO

It goes like this:

```
$Filename = "C:\Program Files (x86)\Microsoft Visual Studio\VB98\Nwind.mdb"
$DBEngine = CreateObject("DAO.$dbEngine.36")
$db = $dbEngine.OpenDatabase($Filename)
```

An ISAM Connection using DAO

It works like this:

```
$Filename = "C:\ISAMS\Text"
$DBEngine = CreateObject("DAO.$dbEngine.36")
$db = $dbEngine.OpenDatabase($Filename, false, false, "Text;hdr=yes;")
```

And the Query:

```
$rs = db.OpenRecordset("Select * from [Myfile.csv]")
```

Working with DAO

Below are examples of how you open and create an Access database using DAO.

To create a DAO Database:

```
Const dbLangGeneral = ";LANGID=0x0409;CP=1252;COUNTRY=0"
$dbEngine = CreateObject("DAO.$dbEngine.120")
$db = $dbEngine.CreateDatabase("C:\MyFirst.accdb", dbLangGeneral)

$dbEngine = CreateObject("DAO.$dbEngine.36")
$db = $dbEngine.CreateDatabase("C:\MyFirst.mdb", dbLangGeneral)

$dbEngine = CreateObject("DAO.$dbEngine.35")
$db = $dbEngine.CreateDatabase("C:\MyFirst.mdb", dbLangGeneral)
```

To Open the database:

```
$dbEngine = CreateObject("DAO.$dbEngine.120")
$db = $dbEngine.OpenDatabase("C:\MyFirst.accdb")

$dbEngine = CreateObject("DAO.$dbEngine.36")
$db = $dbEngine.OpenDatabase("C:\MyFirst.mdb")

$dbEngine = CreateObject("DAO.$dbEngine.35")
$db = $dbEngine.OpenDatabase("C:\MyFirst.mdb")
```

Create and populate Table:

```
$tbldef = $db.CreateTableDef("Process_Properties")
For Each $prop in $ob.Properties_
                    $fld = tbldef.CreateField($Prop.Name, 12)
                    $fld.AllowZeroLength = true
                    $tbldef.Fields.Append($fld)
Next
db.TableDefs.Append($tbldef)
```

Open a Recordset:

```
$rs = $db.OpenRecordset("Select * From Processes_Properties", Exclusive:=False)
```

Or:

```
$rs = $db.OpenRecordset("Processes_Properties")
$objs = $ob.Instances_
For Each $obj in $objs
                    Call $rs.AddNew()
                    For Each $prop in $obj.Properties_
                    $rs.fields($prop.Name).Value = GetValue($prop.Name, $obj)
                    Next
                    Call $rs.Update()
Next
```

Putting it all together

You start off with the DAO.DBEngine you have installed on your computer:
In the case of DAO.DBEngine.35:

$DAODBEngine = CreateObject("DAO.DBEngine.35")

In the case of DAO.DBEngine.36:

$DAODBEngine = CreateObject("DAO.DBEngine.36")

In the case of DAO.DBEngine.120:

$DAODBEngine = CreateObject("DAO.DBEngine.120")

Then you create the database:

```
$dbName = "C:\DAODatabase.mdb"
$dbLangGeneral =";LANGID=0x0409;CP=1252;COUNTRY=0"
$dbVersion40 = 64
```

```
$db = $dao.CreateDatabase($dbName, $dbLangGeneral, dbVersion40)
```

Then you create a table including a tablename:

```
$tbldef = $db.CreateTableDef("Win32_Process_Properties")
```

Then you create your fields using the new table's ability to do it, set some properties, and the append the collection with the new field:

```
$fld = $tbldef.CreateField("Name", 12)
$fld.AllowZeroLength = $true
$tbldef.Fields.Append($fld)
```

Once done, you append the collection of TableDefs.

```
$db.TableDefs.Append($tbldef)
```

Now you're ready to populate the Recordset:

```
$rs = db.OpenRecordset("Win32_Process_Properties")
```

You are now read to start adding information:

```
$rs.AddNew()
```

```
$rs.Fields[The name of the field].Value = The value you want to add
```

For as many fields you created.
When you have finished populating the fields in the first row, you tell the recordset to update:

```
$rs.Update()
```

Continue this cycle until you are done. When you are, close the recordset

```
$rs.Close()
$db.Close()
```

Okay, so let's get this show on the road.

```
$dbName = "C:\DAODatabase.mdb"
$dbLangGeneral =";LANGID=0x0409;CP=1252;COUNTRY=0"
$dbVersion40 = 64
$db

$svc = GetObject("winmgmts:[locale=MS-409]\\.\root\cimv2")
$svc.Security_.AuthenticationLevel = 6
$svc.Security_.ImpersonationLevel= 3
$objs = $svc.InstancesOf("Win32_Process")

$fso = CreateObject("Scripting.FileSystemObject")
if($fso.FileExists($dbName) = false)
$db = $dao.CreateDatabase($dbName, $dbLangGeneral, dbVersion40)
    $tbldef = $db.CreateTableDef("Win32_Process")
$obj = $objs.ItemIndex(0)
For Each($prop in $obj.Properties_)
   $fld = $tbldef.CreateField($prop.Name, 12)
   $fld.AllowZeroLength = $true
   $tbldef.Fields.Append($fld)
Next
    $db.TableDefs.Append($tbldef)
   $rs = db.OpenRecordset("Win32_Process")
   For Each($obj in $objs)
      $rs.AddNew()
      For Each($prop in $obj.Properties_)
     $rs.Fields[$prop.Name].Value = GetValue($prop.Name, $obj)
  Next
  $rs.Update()
   Next
EndIf
```

And there you go.

Working with Access

The four ways you can create an Access Database through automation:

1. $oAccess.NewCurrentDatabase("C:\test\Myfirst.mdb", 9)
2. $oAccess.NewCurrentDatabase("C:\test\Myfirst.mdb", 10)
3. $oAccess.NewCurrentDatabase("C:\test\Myfirst.accdb", 12)
4. $oAccess.NewCurrentDatabase("C:\test\Myfirst.accdb", 0)

There are two types of Access Database extensions, as shown below:

1. $oAccess.OpenCurrentDatabase("C:\test\Myfirst.mdb")
2. $oAccess.OpenCurrentDatabase ("C:\test\Myfirst.accdb")

```
$oAccess = CreateObject("Access.Application")
$oAccess.Visible = true;
```

Save this as "Access.kix" and then run it.
What will happen, if Access is installed on your machine is it will flash up on the screen and go away. In truth, this is expected behavior because the program that asked for it went stopped running and is no longer around. To prevent this from happening, I added a MessageBox at the end of the routine so that I could assure the code ran as expected.
Here's that code:

```
$rs1 = CreateObject("ADODB.Recordset")
$rs1.ActiveConnection = "Provider=Microsoft.Jet.OLEDB.4.0;Data
Source=C:\NWind.mdb"
$rs1.CursorLocation = 3
$rs1.LockType = 3
$rs1.Source = "Select * from [Products]"
$rs1.Open()
```

```
$oAccess = CreateObject("Access.Application")
$oAccess.Visible = 1

$fso = CreateObject("Scripting.FileSystemObject")
if($fso.FileExists("C:\Myfirst.mdb") = false)
   $oAccess.NewCurrentDatabase("C:\Myfirst.mdb", 10)
   $db = $oAccess.CurrentDb
   $tbldef = $db.CreateTableDef("Products")

   For $x = 0 to $rs1.Fields.Count-1
      $fld = $tbldef.CreateField($rs1.Fields($x).Name, 12)
      $fld.AllowZeroLength = true
      $tbldef.Fields.Append($fld)
   Next
   $db.TableDefs.Append($tbldef)

   $rs1.MoveLast()
   $rs1.MoveFirst()

   $rs = $db.OpenRecordset("Products")

   while($rs1.eof = false)

      $rs.AddNew()

      For $x = 0 to $rs1.Fields.Count-1
         $rs.Fields($x).Value = $rs1.Fields($x).Value
      Next
      $rs.Update()
      $rs1.MoveNext()
   loop
endif
MessageBox("Click here when you're satisfied.", "Kixtart")
```

The Database, before:

CocosCreator	3/29/2018 5:55 AM	File folder	
inetpub	1/2/2018 6:55 AM	File folder	
NVIDIA	12/19/2017 8:57 PM	File folder	
PerfLogs	8/22/2013 8:52 AM	File folder	
Perl64	3/29/2018 9:25 PM	File folder	
Program Files	3/29/2018 1:55 PM	File folder	
Program Files (x86)	3/29/2018 4:43 PM	File folder	
Python27	3/29/2018 4:39 AM	File folder	
Python27amd64	3/29/2018 4:26 AM	File folder	
Python35	3/29/2018 10:21 PM	File folder	
Users	12/19/2017 7:50 PM	File folder	
Windows	3/29/2018 6:10 PM	File folder	
NWIND	3/30/2018 11:30 PM	Microsoft Access ...	1,836 KB
Stuff	4/4/2018 2:07 PM	File folder	

The Database, after:

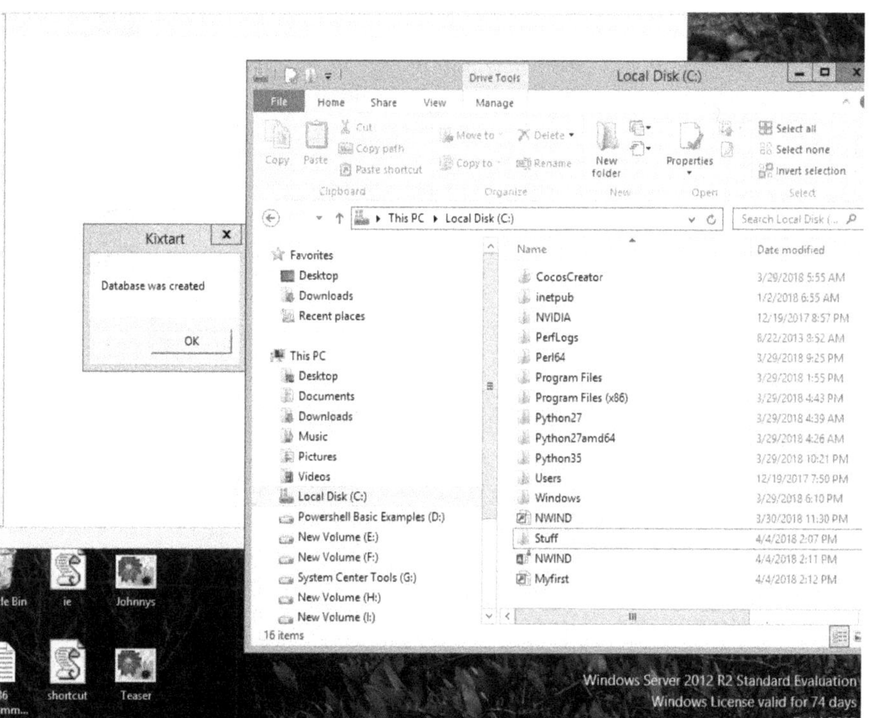

Table, has been created:

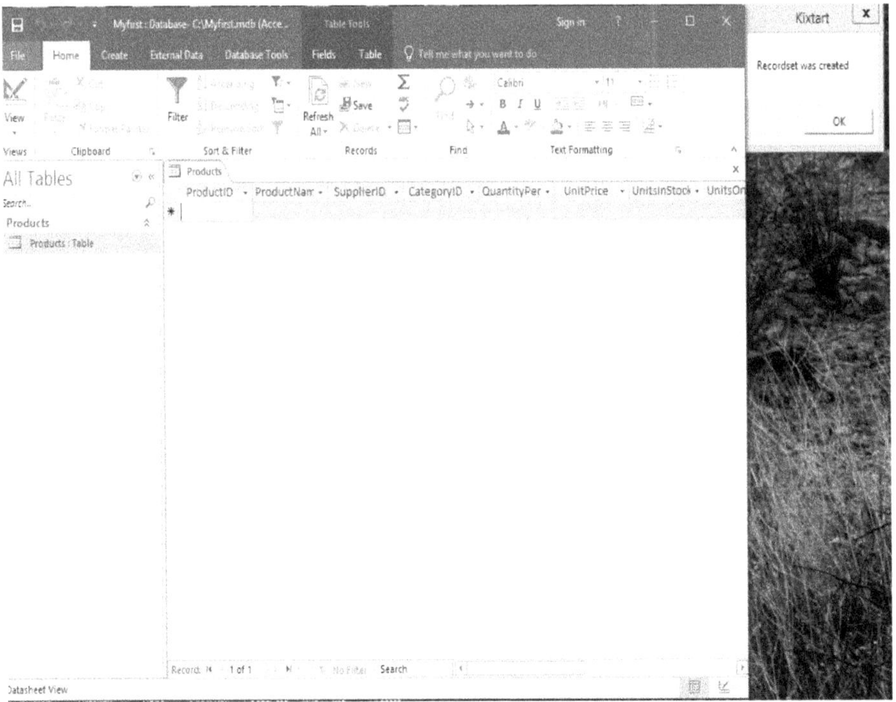

The table has been populated:

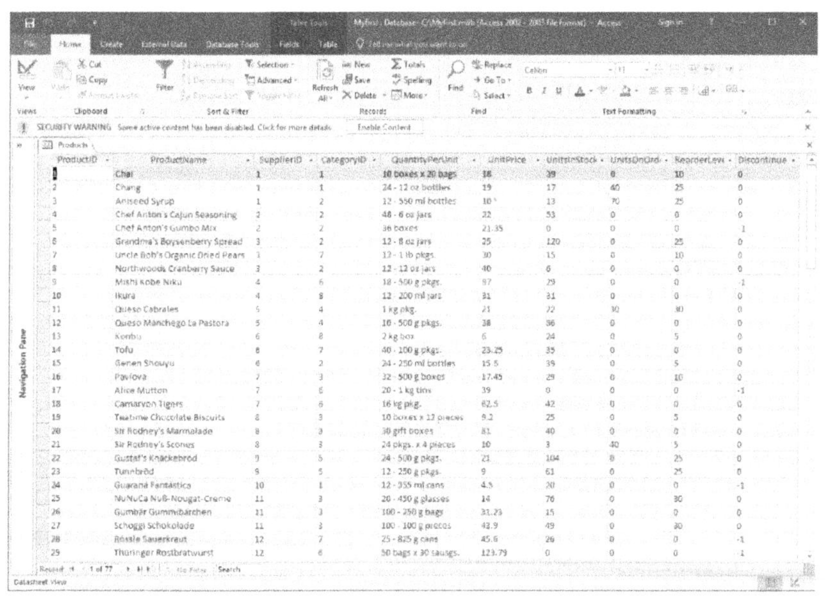

Making Access Work For you

```
$oAccess = CreateObject("Access.Application")
$oAccess.Visible = 1
$oAccess.OpenCurrentDatabase("C:\Myfirst.mdb")
$db = $oAccess.CurrentDb()
$rs = $db.OpenRecordset(“Products”)
$ws = CreateObject("WScript.Shell")
$fso = CreateObject("Scripting.FileSystemObject")
$txtstream = $fso.OpenTextFile("C:\NWIND.html", 2, true, -2)
$txtstream.WriteLine("<html>")
$txtstream.WriteLine("<head>")
$txtstream.WriteLine("<title>Products</title>")
$txtstream.WriteLine("</head>")
$txtstream.WriteLine("<body bgcolor=#333333>")
$txtstream.WriteLine("<center>")
$txtstream.WriteLine("<table colspacing=3 colpadding=3>")
$txtstream.WriteLine("<tr>")
```

```
$count = $rs.Fields.Count -1
for $x = 0 To $count
   $txtstream.WriteLine("<th>" + $rs.Fields($x).Name  + "</th>")
Next
$txtstream.WriteLine("</tr>")
$rs.MoveLast()
$rs.MoveFirst()
while($rs.eof = false)
   $txtstream.WriteLine("<tr>")
   for $x=0 To $Count
      $txtstream.WriteLine("<td>" + $rs.Fields($x).Value  + "</td>")
   Next
   $txtstream.WriteLine("</tr>")
   $rs.MoveNext()
Loop
$txtstream.WriteLine("</table>")
$txtstream.WriteLine("</html>")
$txtstream.close
```

ADO in action

```
$cn = CreateObject("ADODB.Connection")
$cmd = CreateObject("ADODB.Command")
$rs = CreateObject("ADODB.Recordset")

$cn.ConnectionString = "Provider=Microsoft.Jet.OLEDB.4.0;Data
Source=C:\NWIND.MDB;"
$cn.Open()

$rs.ActiveConnection = $cn
$rs.LockType = 3
$rs.CursorLocation = 3
$rs.Source = "Select * from [Products]"
$rs.Open()

$ws = CreateObject("WScript.Shell")
$fso = CreateObject("Scripting.FileSystemObject")
$txtstream = $fso.OpenTextFile("C:\NWIND.html", 2, true, -2)
$txtstream.WriteLine("<html>")
$txtstream.WriteLine("<head>")
$txtstream.WriteLine("<title>Products</title>")
$txtstream.WriteLine("</head>")
$txtstream.WriteLine("<body bgcolor=#333333>")
$txtstream.WriteLine("<center>")
$txtstream.WriteLine("<table colspacing=3 colpadding=3>")
$txtstream.WriteLine("<tr>")
$count = $rs.Fields.Count -1
for $x = 0 To $count
   $txtstream.WriteLine("<th>" + $rs.Fields($x).Name  + "</th>")
Next
```

```
$txtstream.WriteLine("</tr>")
$rs.MoveLast()
$rs.MoveFirst()
while($rs.eof = false)
   $txtstream.WriteLine("<tr>")
   for $x=0 To $Count
$txtstream.WriteLine("<td>" + $rs.Fields($x).Value  + "</td>")
   Next
   $txtstream.WriteLine("</tr>")
   $rs.MoveNext()

Loop
$txtstream.WriteLine("</table>")
$txtstream.WriteLine("</html>")


$txtstream.close
```

DAO in action

```
$dbEngine = CreateObject("DAO.DBEngine.36")
$db = $dbEngine.OpenDatabase("C:\Nwind.mdb")
$rs = $db.OpenRecordset("Products")

$ws = CreateObject("WScript.Shell")
$fso = CreateObject("Scripting.FileSystemObject")
$txtstream = $fso.OpenTextFile("C:\NWIND.html", 2, true, -2)
$txtstream.WriteLine("<html>")
$txtstream.WriteLine("<head>")
$txtstream.WriteLine("<title>Products</title>")
$txtstream.WriteLine("</head>")
$txtstream.WriteLine("<body bgcolor=#333333>")
$txtstream.WriteLine("<center>")
$txtstream.WriteLine("<table colspacing=3 colpadding=3>")
$txtstream.WriteLine("<tr>")
$count = $rs.Fields.Count -1
for $x = 0 To $count
   $txtstream.WriteLine("<th>" + $rs.Fields($x).Name  + "</th>")
Next
$txtstream.WriteLine("</tr>")
$rs.MoveLast()
$rs.MoveFirst()

while($rs.eof = false)
   $txtstream.WriteLine("<tr>")
   for $x=0 To $Count
      $txtstream.WriteLine("<td>" + $rs.Fields($x).Value  + "</td>")
   Next
   $txtstream.WriteLine("</tr>")
```

```
  $rs.MoveNext()
Loop
$txtstream.WriteLine("</table>")
$txtstream.WriteLine("</html>")
$txtstream.close
```

Using WMI to create a spreadsheet

Horizontal rendering

```
$oExcel = CreateObject("Excel.Application")
$oExcel.Visible = true
$wb = $oExcel.WorkBooks.Add()
$ws = $wb.WorkSheets(1)
$ws.Name = "Win32_Process"

$l = CreateObject("WbemScripting.SWbemLocator")
$svc = $l.ConnectServer(".", "root\cimv2")
$svc.Security_.AuthenticationLevel = 6
$svc.Security_.ImpersonationLevel = 3
$objs = $svc.InstancesOf("Win32_Process")

$v=0
$w = 2

For Each $obj in $objs
   If $v = 0
      For Each $prop in $obj.Properties_
         $ws.Cells(1, ($v+1)).Value =  $prop.Name
         $v=$v+1
      Next
   Endif
```

```
    $v =1
    For Each $prop in $obj.Properties_
      $ws.Cells(($w), ($v)).Value =  GetValue($prop.Name, $obj)
      $v=$v+1
    Next
    $w=$w+1
  Next
$ws.Columns.HorizontalAlignment = -4131
$ws.Columns.Autofit()
```

And here's the output:

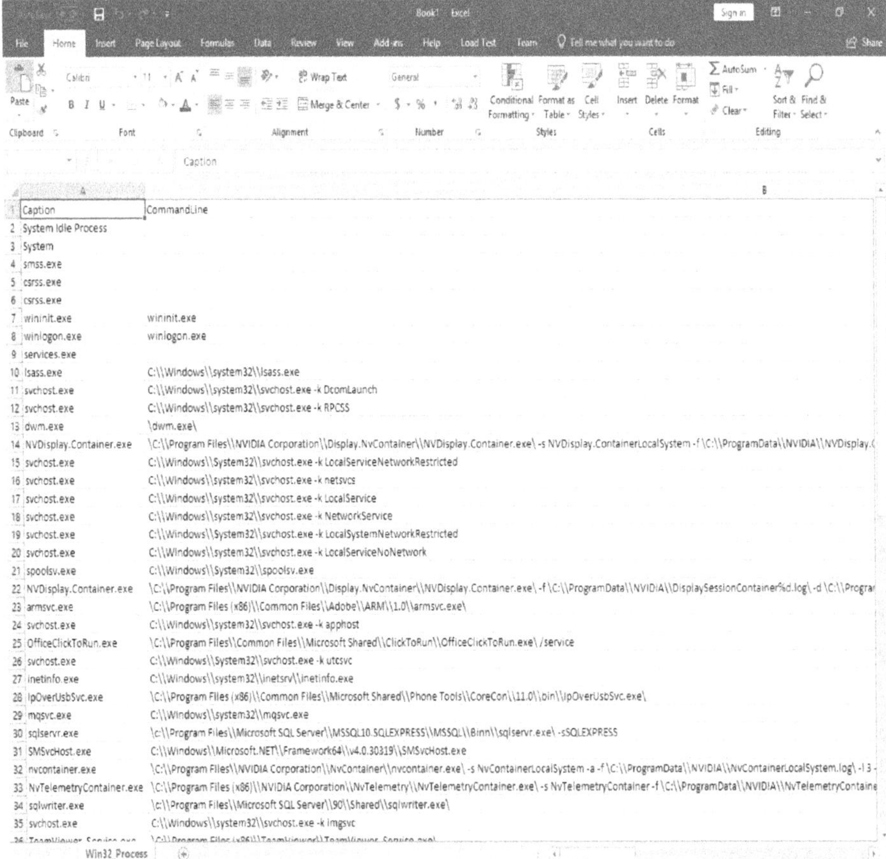

	A	B
1	Caption	CommandLine
2	System Idle Process	
3	System	
4	smss.exe	
5	csrss.exe	
6	csrss.exe	
7	wininit.exe	wininit.exe
8	winlogon.exe	winlogon.exe
9	services.exe	
10	lsass.exe	C:\\Windows\\system32\\lsass.exe
11	svchost.exe	C:\\Windows\\system32\\svchost.exe -k DcomLaunch
12	svchost.exe	C:\\Windows\\system32\\svchost.exe -k RPCSS
13	dwm.exe	\dwm.exe\
14	NVDisplay.Container.exe	\C:\\Program Files\\NVIDIA Corporation\\Display.NvContainer\\NVDisplay.Container.exe\ -s NVDisplay.ContainerLocalSystem -f \C:\\ProgramData\\NVIDIA\\NVDisplay.(
15	svchost.exe	C:\\Windows\\System32\\svchost.exe -k LocalServiceNetworkRestricted
16	svchost.exe	C:\\Windows\\system32\\svchost.exe -k netsvcs
17	svchost.exe	C:\\Windows\\system32\\svchost.exe -k LocalService
18	svchost.exe	C:\\Windows\\system32\\svchost.exe -k NetworkService
19	svchost.exe	C:\\Windows\\System32\\svchost.exe -k LocalSystemNetworkRestricted
20	svchost.exe	C:\\Windows\\system32\\svchost.exe -k LocalServiceNoNetwork
21	spoolsv.exe	C:\\Windows\\System32\\spoolsv.exe
22	NVDisplay.Container.exe	\C:\\Program Files\\NVIDIA Corporation\\Display.NvContainer\\NVDisplay.Container.exe\ -f \C:\\ProgramData\\NVIDIA\\DisplaySessionContainer%d.log\ -d \C:\\Prograr
23	armsvc.exe	\C:\\Program Files (x86)\\Common Files\\Adobe\\ARM\\1.0\\armsvc.exe\
24	svchost.exe	C:\\Windows\\system32\\svchost.exe -k apphost
25	OfficeClickToRun.exe	\C:\\Program Files\\Common Files\\Microsoft Shared\\ClickToRun\\OfficeClickToRun.exe\ /service
26	svchost.exe	C:\\Windows\\System32\\svchost.exe -k utcsvc
27	inetinfo.exe	C:\\Windows\\system32\\inetsrv\\inetinfo.exe
28	IpOverUsbSvc.exe	\C:\\Program Files (x86)\\Common Files\\Microsoft Shared\\Phone Tools\\CoreCon\\11.0\\bin\\IpOverUsbSvc.exe\
29	mqsvc.exe	C:\\Windows\\system32\\mqsvc.exe
30	sqlservr.exe	\c:\\Program Files\\Microsoft SQL Server\\MSSQL10.SQLEXPRESS\\MSSQL\\Binn\\sqlservr.exe\ -sSQLEXPRESS
31	SMSvcHost.exe	C:\\Windows\\Microsoft.NET\\Framework64\\v4.0.30319\\SMSvcHost.exe
32	nvcontainer.exe	\C:\\Program Files\\NVIDIA Corporation\\NvContainer\\nvcontainer.exe\ -s NvContainerLocalSystem -a -f \C:\\ProgramData\\NVIDIA\\NvContainerLocalSystem.log\ -l 3 -
33	NvTelemetryContainer.exe	\C:\\Program Files (x86)\\NVIDIA Corporation\\NvTelemetry\\NvTelemetryContainer.exe\ -s NvTelemetryContainer -f \C:\\ProgramData\\NVIDIA\\NvTelemetryContaine
34	sqlwriter.exe	\c:\\Program Files\\Microsoft SQL Server\\90\\Shared\\sqlwriter.exe\
35	svchost.exe	C:\\Windows\\system32\\svchost.exe -k imgsvc

Vertical rendering:

```
$oExcel = CreateObject("Excel.Application")
$oExcel.Visible = true
$wb = $oExcel.WorkBooks.Add()
$ws = $wb.WorkSheets(1)
$ws.Name = "Win32_Process"

$l = CreateObject("WbemScripting.SWbemLocator")
$svc = $l.ConnectServer(".", "root\cimv2")
$svc.Security_.AuthenticationLevel = 6
$svc.Security_.ImpersonationLevel = 3
$objs = $svc.InstancesOf("Win32_Process")

$v=0
$w = 2

For Each $obj in $objs
   If $v = 0
      For Each $prop in $obj.Properties_
         $ws.Cells(($v+1), 1).Value =  $prop.Name
         $v=$v+1
      Next
   Endif
   $v =1
   For Each $prop in $obj.Properties_
      $ws.Cells(($v), ($w)).Value =  GetValue($prop.Name, $obj)
      $v=$v+1
   Next
   $w=$w+1
  Next
$ws.Columns.HorizontalAlignment = -4131
$ws.Columns.Autofit()
```

And below is the vertical view:

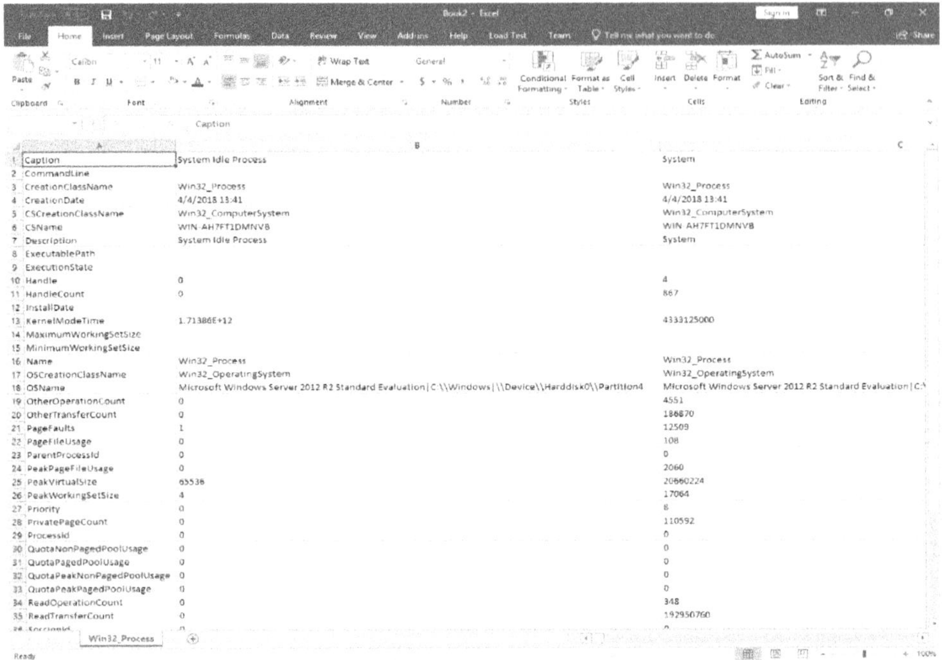

	A	B	C
1	Caption	System Idle Process	System
2	CommandLine		
3	CreationClassName	Win32_Process	Win32_Process
4	CreationDate	4/4/2018 13:41	4/4/2018 13:41
5	CSCreationClassName	Win32_ComputerSystem	Win32_ComputerSystem
6	CSName	WIN-AH7FT1DMNVB	WIN-AH7FT1DMNVB
7	Description	System Idle Process	System
8	ExecutablePath		
9	ExecutionState		
10	Handle	0	4
11	HandleCount	0	867
12	InstallDate		
13	KernelModeTime	1.71386E+12	4333125000
14	MaximumWorkingSetSize		
15	MinimumWorkingSetSize		
16	Name	Win32_Process	Win32_Process
17	OSCreationClassName	Win32_OperatingSystem	Win32_OperatingSystem
18	OSName	Microsoft Windows Server 2012 R2 Standard Evaluation|C:\\Windows|\\Device\\Harddisk0\\Partition4	Microsoft Windows Server 2012 R2 Standard Evaluation|C:\
19	OtherOperationCount	0	4551
20	OtherTransferCount	0	186870
21	PageFaults	1	12509
22	PageFileUsage	0	108
23	ParentProcessId	0	0
24	PeakPageFileUsage	0	2060
25	PeakVirtualSize	65536	20660224
26	PeakWorkingSetSize	4	17064
27	Priority	0	8
28	PrivatePageCount	0	110592
29	ProcessId	0	0
30	QuotaNonPagedPoolUsage	0	0
31	QuotaPagedPoolUsage	0	0
32	QuotaPeakNonPagedPoolUsage	0	0
33	QuotaPeakPagedPoolUsage	0	0
34	ReadOperationCount	0	348
35	ReadTransferCount	0	192950760

Transferring from Access to Excel

Below is the code for the ADO code example in Horizontal format:

```
$oExcel = CreateObject("Excel.Application")
$oExcel.Visible = true
$wb = $oExcel.WorkBooks.Add()
$ws = $wb.WorkSheets(1)
$ws.Name = "Products"


$rs = CreateObject("ADODB.Recordset")
$rs.ActiveConnection = "Provider=Microsoft.Jet.OLEDB.4.0;Data
Source=C:\NWind.mdb"
$rs.CursorLocation = 3
$rs.LockType = 3
$rs.Source = "Select * from [Products]"
$rs.Open()


$count = $rs.Fields.Count -1

$v=2
for $x = 0 To $count
  $ws.Cells.Item(1, ($x+1)).Value = $rs.Fields($x).Name
Next

$rs.MoveLast()
```

```
$rs.MoveFirst()

while($rs.eof = false)
   for $x=0 To $count
      $ws.Cells.Item(($v),($x+1)).Value = $rs.Fields($x).Value
   Next
   $rs.MoveNext()
   $v=$v+1
Loop

$ws.Columns.HorizontalAlignment = -4131
$ws.Columns.Autofit()
```

And here's the view:

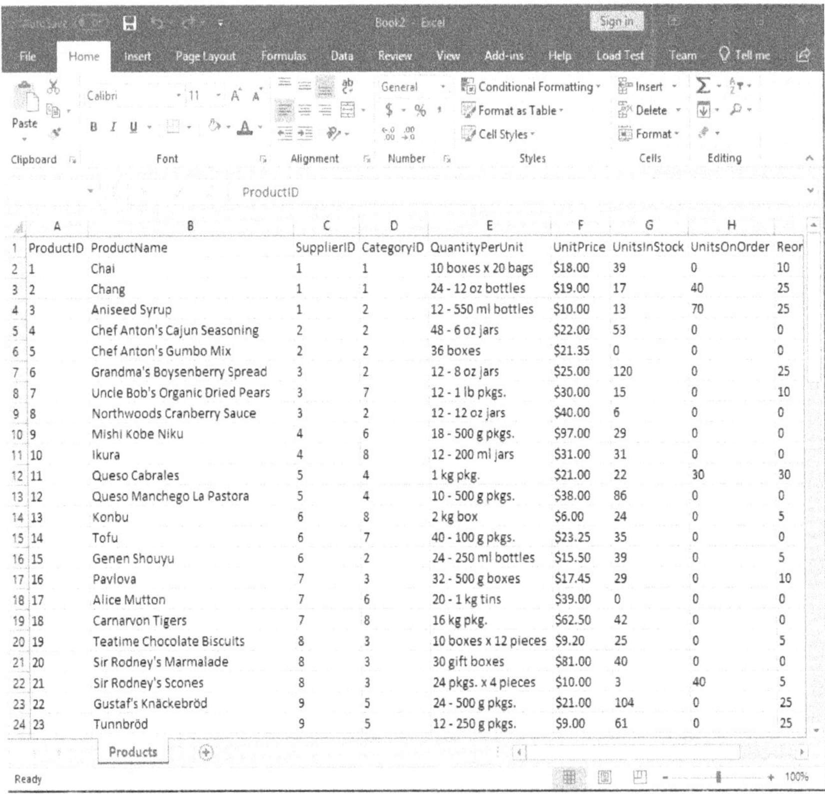

ProductID	ProductName	SupplierID	CategoryID	QuantityPerUnit	UnitPrice	UnitsInStock	UnitsOnOrder	Reor
1	Chai	1	1	10 boxes x 20 bags	$18.00	39	0	10
2	Chang	1	1	24 - 12 oz bottles	$19.00	17	40	25
3	Aniseed Syrup	1	2	12 - 550 ml bottles	$10.00	13	70	25
4	Chef Anton's Cajun Seasoning	2	2	48 - 6 oz jars	$22.00	53	0	0
5	Chef Anton's Gumbo Mix	2	2	36 boxes	$21.35	0	0	0
6	Grandma's Boysenberry Spread	3	2	12 - 8 oz jars	$25.00	120	0	25
7	Uncle Bob's Organic Dried Pears	3	7	12 - 1 lb pkgs.	$30.00	15	0	10
8	Northwoods Cranberry Sauce	3	2	12 - 12 oz jars	$40.00	6	0	0
9	Mishi Kobe Niku	4	6	18 - 500 g pkgs.	$97.00	29	0	0
10	Ikura	4	8	12 - 200 ml jars	$31.00	31	0	0
11	Queso Cabrales	5	4	1 kg pkg.	$21.00	22	30	30
12	Queso Manchego La Pastora	5	4	10 - 500 g pkgs.	$38.00	86	0	0
13	Konbu	6	8	2 kg box	$6.00	24	0	5
14	Tofu	6	7	40 - 100 g pkgs.	$23.25	35	0	0
15	Genen Shouyu	6	2	24 - 250 ml bottles	$15.50	39	0	5
16	Pavlova	7	3	32 - 500 g boxes	$17.45	29	0	10
17	Alice Mutton	7	6	20 - 1 kg tins	$39.00	0	0	0
18	Carnarvon Tigers	7	8	16 kg pkg.	$62.50	42	0	0
19	Teatime Chocolate Biscuits	8	3	10 boxes x 12 pieces	$9.20	25	0	5
20	Sir Rodney's Marmalade	8	3	30 gift boxes	$81.00	40	0	0
21	Sir Rodney's Scones	8	3	24 pkgs. x 4 pieces	$10.00	3	40	5
22	Gustaf's Knäckebröd	9	5	24 - 500 g pkgs.	$21.00	104	0	25
23	Tunnbröd	9	5	12 - 250 g pkgs.	$9.00	61	0	25

Below is the Vertical code:

```
$oExcel = CreateObject("Excel.Application")
$oExcel.Visible = true
$wb = $oExcel.WorkBooks.Add()
$ws = $wb.WorkSheets(1)
$ws.Name = "Products"


$rs = CreateObject("ADODB.Recordset")
$rs.ActiveConnection = "Provider=Microsoft.Jet.OLEDB.4.0;Data
Source=C:\NWind.mdb"
$rs.CursorLocation = 3
$rs.LockType = 3
$rs.Source = "Select * from [Products]"
$rs.Open()


$count = $rs.Fields.Count -1

$v=2
for $x = 0 To $count
  $ws.Cells.Item(($x+1), 1).Value = $rs.Fields($x).Name
Next

$rs.MoveLast()
$rs.MoveFirst()

while($rs.eof = false)
   for $x=0 To $count
      $ws.Cells.Item(($x+1),($v)).Value = $rs.Fields($x).Value
   Next
   $rs.MoveNext()
   $v=$v+1
Loop

$ws.Columns.HorizontalAlignment = -4131
$ws.Columns.Autofit()
```

And below this is the output:

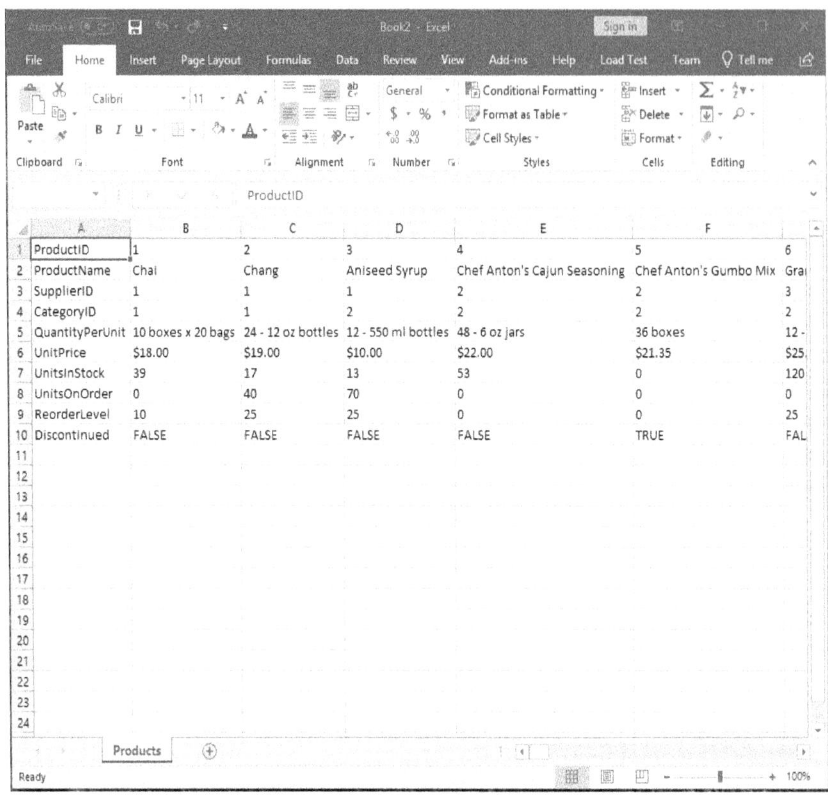

	A	B	C	D	E	F	
1	ProductID	1	2	3	4	5	6
2	ProductName	Chai	Chang	Aniseed Syrup	Chef Anton's Cajun Seasoning	Chef Anton's Gumbo Mix	Grai
3	SupplierID	1	1	1	2	2	3
4	CategoryID	1	1	2	2	2	2
5	QuantityPerUnit	10 boxes x 20 bags	24 - 12 oz bottles	12 - 550 ml bottles	48 - 6 oz jars	36 boxes	12 -
6	UnitPrice	$18.00	$19.00	$10.00	$22.00	$21.35	$25.
7	UnitsInStock	39	17	13	53	0	120
8	UnitsOnOrder	0	40	70	0	0	0
9	ReorderLevel	10	25	25	0	0	25
10	Discontinued	FALSE	FALSE	FALSE	FALSE	TRUE	FAL

Excel Output

One of the issues with using Excel is that you must figure out where, exactly, is the end of the record is. Luckily, you don't have to worry about it if you use the OLEDB provider. The code being presented to you will work to acquire information from an .xls file.

Technically, this is not accessing Excel itself.

Anyway, the idea here is to show you the code using ADO and code using DAO to acquire the same results.

ADO EXAMPLE OF USING AN EXCEL .xls FILE

```
$adOpenStatic = 3
$adLockOptimistic = 3
$adCmdText = 1

$cn = CreateObject("ADODB.Connection")
$cn.ConnectionString = "Provider=Microsoft.Jet.OleDb.4.0;Data
Source=C:\book2.xls;"
$cn.Properties("Extended Properties").Value="Excel 8.0;hdr=yes;"
$cn.Open()


$rs = CreateObject("ADODB.Recordset")
$rs.Open("Select * From [Products$]", $cn, $adOpenStatic, $adLockOptimistic,
$adCmdText)
```

```
$ws = CreateObject("WScript.Shell")
$fso = CreateObject("Scripting.FileSystemObject")
$txtstream = $fso.OpenTextFile("C:\NWIND.html", 2, true, -2)
$txtstream.WriteLine("<html>")
$txtstream.WriteLine("<head>")
$txtstream.WriteLine("<title>Products</title>")
$txtstream.WriteLine("</head>")
$txtstream.WriteLine("<body bgcolor=#333333>")
$txtstream.WriteLine("<center>")
$txtstream.WriteLine("<table colspacing=3 colpadding=3>")
$txtstream.WriteLine("<tr>")
$count = $rs.Fields.Count -1
for $x = 0 To $count
   $txtstream.WriteLine("<th>" + $rs.Fields($x).Name  + "</th>")
Next
$txtstream.WriteLine("</tr>")

$rs.MoveLast()
$rs.MoveFirst()

while($rs.eof = false)

   $txtstream.WriteLine("<tr>")
   for $x=0 To $Count
      $txtstream.WriteLine("<td>" + $rs.Fields($x).Value  + "</td>")
   Next
   $txtstream.WriteLine("</tr>")
   $rs.MoveNext()

Loop
$txtstream.WriteLine("</table>")
$txtstream.WriteLine("</html>")
$txtstream.close
```

HTML report using WMI

Below is a tested, fully functional HTML report generated using Kixtart code.

```
$l = CreateObject("WbemScripting.SWbemLocator")
$svc = $l.ConnectServer(".", "root\cimv2")
$svc.Security_.AuthenticationLevel = 6
$svc.Security_.ImpersonationLevel = 3
$objs = $svc.ExecQuery("Select * From Win32_Process")

$ws = CreateObject("WScript.Shell")
$fso = CreateObject("Scripting.FileSystemObject")
$txtstream = $fso.OpenTextFile("C:\Process.html", 2, true, -2)
$txtstream.WriteLine("<html>")
$txtstream.WriteLine("<head>")
$txtstream.WriteLine("<title>Process</title>")
$txtstream.WriteLine("</head>")
$txtstream.WriteLine("<body bgcolor=#333333>")
$txtstream.WriteLine("<center>")
$txtstream.WriteLine("<table colspacing=3 colpadding=3>")
$obj = $objs.ItemIndex(0)
$txtstream.WriteLine("<tr>")
For Each $prop in $obj.Properties_
  $txtstream.WriteLine("<th>" + $prop.Name  + "</th>")
Next
$txtstream.WriteLine("</tr>")
For Each $obj in $objs
   $txtstream.WriteLine("<tr>")
   For Each $prop in $obj.Properties_
```

```
    $txtstream.WriteLine("<td>" + GetValue($prop.Name, $obj)  + "</td>")
   Next
   $txtstream.WriteLine("</tr>")
Next
$txtstream.WriteLine("</table>")
$txtstream.WriteLine("</html>")
$txtstream.close
```

XML output

The absolute beauty of using XML is it is either correctly created or it is not. Which can pretty cause anyone who isn't bald become one.

Okay, so allow me to explain what the difference is between Attribute XML, Element XML, Element XML for XSL and Schema XML.
Attribute XML is a type of XML which enables you to place a ton of information on one line of XML.
When XML first came out back in 1998, it did not have Attribute XML. It wasn't until after 2000 that Attribute XML was made available. Which made my life with XML much harder to work with.
Attribute XML is fully customizable. But you need to know what you want, where you've placed the node and what needs to be done with that node.
Element XML is a much simpler to work with but doesn't enable you to work each node like it were a column of information. However, sub nodes and the mixture of attributes sprinkled in can make simple complex very quickly.
Both In its simplest of notation, Element XML for XSL and Schema XML use the same Element XML
The Element XML for XSL adds an additional processing instruction at the top of the file. And the Schema XML is an Element XML File that gets converted to a Schema – or definition table – and a lot of Attribute nodes known as z:rows.

Attribute XML

Have you ever wanted to take a name, a datatype, control type, a value, and place it on one line of XML?

I have. We used an excel spreadsheet to do the same until Attribute XML entered the world of XML

Anyway, here's what the code looks like:

```
$crlf = Chr(13) + Chr(10)

$tempstr
$Name
$Value
$v

$l = CreateObject("WbemScripting.SWbemLocator")
$svc = $l.ConnectServer(".", "root\cimv2")
$svc.Security_.AuthenticationLevel = 6
$svc.Security_.ImpersonationLevel = 3
$objs = $svc.InstancesOf("Win32_Process")

$ws = CreateObject("WScript.Shell")
$fso = CreateObject("Scripting.FileSystemObject")
$v=0

$txtstream = $fso.OpenTextFile("C:\Win32_Process.xml", 2, True, -2)
$txtstream.WriteLine("<?xml version='1.0' encoding='iso-8859-1'?>")
$txtstream.WriteLine("<data>")


For Each $obj in $objs
   $txtstream.WriteLine("<win32_process>")
   For Each $prop in $obj.Properties_
      $txtstream.WriteLine("<property name = " + chr(34) + $prop.Name + chr(34) +
" datatype= " + chr(34) + "string" + chr(34) + " controltype = " + chr(34) +
"Textbox" + chr(34) + " value=" + chr(34) + GetValue($prop.Name, $obj) + chr(34)+
"/>")
   Next
   $txtstream.WriteLine("</win32_process>")
Next
$txtstream.WriteLine("</data>")
$txtstream.Close
```

And here is a partial view of the output:

```
- <win32_process>
    <property name="Caption" datatype="string" controltype="Textbox" value="System Idle Process"/>
    <property name="CommandLine" datatype="string" controltype="Textbox" value=""/>
    <property name="CreationClassName" datatype="string" controltype="Textbox" value="Win32_Process"/>
    <property name="CreationDate" datatype="string" controltype="Textbox" value="04/04/2018 13:41:49"/>
    <property name="CSCreationClassName" datatype="string" controltype="Textbox" value="Win32_ComputerSystem"/>
    <property name="CSName" datatype="string" controltype="Textbox" value="WIN-AH7FT1DMNVB"/>
    <property name="Description" datatype="string" controltype="Textbox" value="System Idle Process"/>
    <property name="ExecutablePath" datatype="string" controltype="Textbox" value=""/>
    <property name="ExecutionState" datatype="string" controltype="Textbox" value=""/>
    <property name="Handle" datatype="string" controltype="Textbox" value="0"/>
    <property name="HandleCount" datatype="string" controltype="Textbox" value="0"/>
    <property name="InstallDate" datatype="string" controltype="Textbox" value=""/>
    <property name="KernelModeTime" datatype="string" controltype="Textbox" value="6600245468750"/>
    <property name="MaximumWorkingSetSize" datatype="string" controltype="Textbox" value=""/>
    <property name="MinimumWorkingSetSize" datatype="string" controltype="Textbox" value=""/>
    <property name="Name" datatype="string" controltype="Textbox" value="Win32_Process"/>
    <property name="OSCreationClassName" datatype="string" controltype="Textbox" value="Win32_OperatingSystem"/>
    <property name="OSName" datatype="string" controltype="Textbox" value="Microsoft Windows Server 2012 R2 Standard Evaluation|C:\\Windows|\\Device\\Harddisk0\\Partition4"/>
    <property name="OtherOperationCount" datatype="string" controltype="Textbox" value="0"/>
    <property name="OtherTransferCount" datatype="string" controltype="Textbox" value="0"/>
    <property name="PageFaults" datatype="string" controltype="Textbox" value="1"/>
    <property name="PageFileUsage" datatype="string" controltype="Textbox" value="0"/>
    <property name="ParentProcessId" datatype="string" controltype="Textbox" value="0"/>
    <property name="PeakPageFileUsage" datatype="string" controltype="Textbox" value="0"/>
    <property name="PeakVirtualSize" datatype="string" controltype="Textbox" value="65536"/>
    <property name="PeakWorkingSetSize" datatype="string" controltype="Textbox" value="4"/>
    <property name="Priority" datatype="string" controltype="Textbox" value="0"/>
    <property name="PrivatePageCount" datatype="string" controltype="Textbox" value="0"/>
    <property name="ProcessId" datatype="string" controltype="Textbox" value="0"/>
    <property name="QuotaNonPagedPoolUsage" datatype="string" controltype="Textbox" value="0"/>
    <property name="QuotaPagedPoolUsage" datatype="string" controltype="Textbox" value="0"/>
    <property name="QuotaPeakNonPagedPoolUsage" datatype="string" controltype="Textbox" value="0"/>
    <property name="QuotaPeakPagedPoolUsage" datatype="string" controltype="Textbox" value="0"/>
    <property name="ReadOperationCount" datatype="string" controltype="Textbox" value="0"/>
    <property name="ReadTransferCount" datatype="string" controltype="Textbox" value="0"/>
    <property name="SessionId" datatype="string" controltype="Textbox" value="0"/>
    <property name="Status" datatype="string" controltype="Textbox" value=""/>
    <property name="TerminationDate" datatype="string" controltype="Textbox" value=""/>
    <property name="ThreadCount" datatype="string" controltype="Textbox" value="8"/>
    <property name="UserModeTime" datatype="string" controltype="Textbox" value="0"/>
    <property name="VirtualSize" datatype="string" controltype="Textbox" value="65536"/>
    <property name="WindowsVersion" datatype="string" controltype="Textbox" value="6.3.9600"/>
    <property name="WorkingSetSize" datatype="string" controltype="Textbox" value="4"/>
    <property name="WriteOperationCount" datatype="string" controltype="Textbox" value="0"/>
    <property name="WriteTransferCount" datatype="string" controltype="Textbox" value="0"/>
  </win32_process>
```


Below is what the output looks like in excel:

```
- <win32_process>
    <property name="Caption" datatype="string" controltype="Textbox" value="System Idle Process"/>
    <property name="CommandLine" datatype="string" controltype="Textbox" value=""/>
    <property name="CreationClassName" datatype="string" controltype="Textbox" value="Win32_Process"/>
    <property name="CreationDate" datatype="string" controltype="Textbox" value="04/04/2018 13:41:49"/>
    <property name="CSCreationClassName" datatype="string" controltype="Textbox" value="Win32_ComputerSystem"/>
    <property name="CSName" datatype="string" controltype="Textbox" value="WIN-AH7FT1DMNVB"/>
    <property name="Description" datatype="string" controltype="Textbox" value="System Idle Process"/>
    <property name="ExecutablePath" datatype="string" controltype="Textbox" value=""/>
    <property name="ExecutionState" datatype="string" controltype="Textbox" value=""/>
    <property name="Handle" datatype="string" controltype="Textbox" value="0"/>
    <property name="HandleCount" datatype="string" controltype="Textbox" value="0"/>
    <property name="InstallDate" datatype="string" controltype="Textbox" value=""/>
    <property name="KernelModeTime" datatype="string" controltype="Textbox" value="6600245468750"/>
    <property name="MaximumWorkingSetSize" datatype="string" controltype="Textbox" value=""/>
    <property name="MinimumWorkingSetSize" datatype="string" controltype="Textbox" value=""/>
    <property name="Name" datatype="string" controltype="Textbox" value="Win32_Process"/>
    <property name="OSCreationClassName" datatype="string" controltype="Textbox" value="Win32_OperatingSystem"/>
    <property name="OSName" datatype="string" controltype="Textbox" value="Microsoft Windows Server 2012 R2 Standard Evaluation|C:\Windows|\Device\Harddisk0\Partition4"/>
    <property name="OtherOperationCount" datatype="string" controltype="Textbox" value="0"/>
    <property name="OtherTransferCount" datatype="string" controltype="Textbox" value="0"/>
    <property name="PageFaults" datatype="string" controltype="Textbox" value="1"/>
    <property name="PageFileUsage" datatype="string" controltype="Textbox" value="0"/>
    <property name="ParentProcessId" datatype="string" controltype="Textbox" value="0"/>
    <property name="PeakPageFileUsage" datatype="string" controltype="Textbox" value="0"/>
    <property name="PeakVirtualSize" datatype="string" controltype="Textbox" value="65536"/>
    <property name="PeakWorkingSetSize" datatype="string" controltype="Textbox" value="4"/>
    <property name="Priority" datatype="string" controltype="Textbox" value="0"/>
    <property name="PrivatePageCount" datatype="string" controltype="Textbox" value="0"/>
    <property name="ProcessId" datatype="string" controltype="Textbox" value="0"/>
    <property name="QuotaNonPagedPoolUsage" datatype="string" controltype="Textbox" value="0"/>
    <property name="QuotaPagedPoolUsage" datatype="string" controltype="Textbox" value="0"/>
    <property name="QuotaPeakNonPagedPoolUsage" datatype="string" controltype="Textbox" value="0"/>
    <property name="QuotaPeakPagedPoolUsage" datatype="string" controltype="Textbox" value="0"/>
    <property name="ReadOperationCount" datatype="string" controltype="Textbox" value="0"/>
    <property name="ReadTransferCount" datatype="string" controltype="Textbox" value="0"/>
    <property name="SessionId" datatype="string" controltype="Textbox" value="0"/>
    <property name="Status" datatype="string" controltype="Textbox" value=""/>
    <property name="TerminationDate" datatype="string" controltype="Textbox" value=""/>
    <property name="ThreadCount" datatype="string" controltype="Textbox" value="8"/>
    <property name="UserModeTime" datatype="string" controltype="Textbox" value="0"/>
    <property name="VirtualSize" datatype="string" controltype="Textbox" value="65536"/>
    <property name="WindowsVersion" datatype="string" controltype="Textbox" value="6.3.9600"/>
    <property name="WorkingSetSize" datatype="string" controltype="Textbox" value="4"/>
    <property name="WriteOperationCount" datatype="string" controltype="Textbox" value="0"/>
    <property name="WriteTransferCount" datatype="string" controltype="Textbox" value="0"/>
  </win32_process>
```

Element XML

I enjoy working with XML because it is easy to write – when you have the code already available, it is just a few line changes.
Okay, so here's the code:

```
$crlf = Chr(13) + Chr(10)

$tempstr
$Name
$Value
$v

$l = CreateObject("WbemScripting.SWbemLocator")
$svc = $l.ConnectServer(".", "root\cimv2")
$svc.Security_.AuthenticationLevel = 6
$svc.Security_.ImpersonationLevel = 3
$objs = $svc.InstancesOf("Win32_Process")

$ws = CreateObject("WScript.Shell")
$fso = CreateObject("Scripting.FileSystemObject")
$v=0

$txtstream = $fso.OpenTextFile($ws.CurrentDirectory + "\Win32_Process.xml", 2, True, -2)
$txtstream.WriteLine("<?xml version='1.0' encoding='iso-8859-1'?>")
$txtstream.WriteLine("<data>")

For Each $obj in $objs
   $txtstream.WriteLine("<win32_process>")
   For Each $prop in $obj.Properties_
      $txtstream.WriteLine("<" + $prop.Name + ">" + GetValue($prop.Name, $obj) + "</" + $prop.Name + ">")
   Next
   $txtstream.WriteLine("</win32_process>")
Next
$txtstream.WriteLine("</data>")
$txtstream.Close
```

```
$cn = CreateObject("ADODB.Connection")
$cn.Open("Provider=MSXML2.DSOControl;")

$rs = CreateObject("ADODB.Recordset")

$rs.Open($ws.CurrentDirectory + "\Win32_Process.xml", $cn)

$rs.Save($ws.CurrentDirectory + "\Process_Schema.xml", 1)
```

And here's a partial view of the output:


```
<?xml version="1.0" encoding="ISO-8859-1"?>
- <data>
  - <Win32_Process>
      <Caption>System Idle Process</Caption>
      <CommandLine/>
      <CreationClassName>Win32_Process</CreationClassName>
      <CreationDate>20170714173009.696508-420</CreationDate>
      <CSCreationClassName>Win32_ComputerSystem</CSCreationClassName>
      <CSName>WIN-0BPMHO8BTH1</CSName>
      <Description>System Idle Process</Description>
      <ExecutablePath/>
      <ExecutionState/>
      <Handle>0</Handle>
      <HandleCount/>
      <InstallDate/>
      <KernelModeTime>3031410000000</KernelModeTime>
      <MaximumWorkingSetSize/>
      <MinimumWorkingSetSize/>
      <Name>Win32_Process</Name>
      <OSCreationClassName>Win32_OperatingSystem</OSCreationClassName>
      <OSName>Microsoft Windows Server 2012 R2 Datacenter Evaluation|C:\\Windows|\\Device\\Harddisk1\\Partition4</OSName>
      <OtherOperationCount>0</OtherOperationCount>
      <OtherTransferCount>0</OtherTransferCount>
      <PageFaults/>
      <PageFileUsage/>
      <ParentProcessId/>
      <PeakPageFileUsage/>
      <PeakVirtualSize>65536</PeakVirtualSize>
      <PeakWorkingSetSize/>
      <Priority/>
      <PrivatePageCount>0</PrivatePageCount>
      <ProcessId/>
      <QuotaNonPagedPoolUsage/>
      <QuotaPagedPoolUsage/>
      <QuotaPeakNonPagedPoolUsage/>
      <QuotaPeakPagedPoolUsage/>
      <ReadOperationCount>0</ReadOperationCount>
      <ReadTransferCount>0</ReadTransferCount>
      <SessionId/>
      <Status/>
      <TerminationDate/>
      <ThreadCount/>
      <UserModeTime>0</UserModeTime>
      <VirtualSize>65536</VirtualSize>
      <WindowsVersion>6.3.9600</WindowsVersion>
      <WorkingSetSize/>
      <WriteOperationCount>0</WriteOperationCount>
      <WriteTransferCount>0</WriteTransferCount>
    </Win32_Process>
```


And here's what it looks like in excel:

1	Caption	CommandLine	CreationClassName
2	System Idle Process		Win32_Process
3	System		Win32_Process
4	smss.exe		Win32_Process
5	csrss.exe		Win32_Process
6	csrss.exe		Win32_Process
7	wininit.exe	wininit.exe	Win32_Process
8	winlogon.exe	winlogon.exe	Win32_Process
9	services.exe		Win32_Process
10	lsass.exe	C:\\Windows\\system32\\lsass.exe	Win32_Process
11	svchost.exe	C:\\Windows\\system32\\svchost.exe -k DcomLaunch	Win32_Process
12	svchost.exe	C:\\Windows\\system32\\svchost.exe -k RPCSS	Win32_Process
13	dwm.exe	\dwm.exe\	Win32_Process
14	NVDisplay.Container.exe	\C:\\Program Files\\NVIDIA Corporation\\Display.NvContainer\\NVDisplay.Container.exe\	Win32_Process
15	svchost.exe	C:\\Windows\\System32\\svchost.exe -k LocalServiceNetworkRestricted	Win32_Process
16	svchost.exe	C:\\Windows\\system32\\svchost.exe -k netsvcs	Win32_Process
17	svchost.exe	C:\\Windows\\system32\\svchost.exe -k LocalService	Win32_Process
18	svchost.exe	C:\\Windows\\system32\\svchost.exe -k NetworkService	Win32_Process
19	svchost.exe	C:\\Windows\\System32\\svchost.exe -k LocalSystemNetworkRestricted	Win32_Process
20	svchost.exe	C:\\Windows\\system32\\svchost.exe -k LocalServiceNoNetwork	Win32_Process
21	spoolsv.exe	C:\\Windows\\System32\\spoolsv.exe	Win32_Process
22	NVDisplay.Container.exe	\C:\\Program Files\\NVIDIA Corporation\\Display.NvContainer\\NVDisplay.Container.exe\	Win32_Process
23	armsvc.exe	\C:\\Program Files (x86)\\Common Files\\Adobe\\ARM\\1.0\\armsvc.exe\	Win32_Process
24	svchost.exe	C:\\Windows\\system32\\svchost.exe -k apphost	Win32_Process
25	OfficeClickToRun.exe	\C:\\Program Files\\Common Files\\Microsoft Shared\\ClickToRun\\OfficeClickToRun.exe\	Win32_Process
26	svchost.exe	C:\\Windows\\System32\\svchost.exe -k utcsvc	Win32_Process
27	inetinfo.exe	C:\\Windows\\system32\\inetsrv\\inetinfo.exe	Win32_Process
28	IpOverUsbSvc.exe	\C:\\Program Files (x86)\\Common Files\\Microsoft Shared\\Phone Tools\\CoreCon\\11.0\\	Win32_Process
29	mqsvc.exe	C:\\Windows\\system32\\mqsvc.exe	Win32_Process
30	sqlservr.exe	\c:\\Program Files\\Microsoft SQL Server\\MSSQL10.SQLEXPRESS\\MSSQL\\Binn\\sqlservr.e	Win32_Process
31	SMSvcHost.exe	C:\\Windows\\Microsoft.NET\\Framework64\\v4.0.30319\\SMSvcHost.exe	Win32_Process
32	nvcontainer.exe	\C:\\Program Files\\NVIDIA Corporation\\NvContainer\\nvcontainer.exe\ -s NvContainerLo	Win32_Process
33	NvTelemetryContainer.exe	\C:\\Program Files (x86)\\NVIDIA Corporation\\NvTelemetry\\NvTelemetryContainer.exe\	Win32_Process
34	sqlwriter.exe	\c:\\Program Files\\Microsoft SQL Server\\90\\Shared\\sqlwriter.exe\	Win32_Process
35	svchost.exe	C:\\Windows\\system32\\svchost.exe -k imgsvc	Win32_Process

Element XML for XSL

One line turns the Element XML into Element XML for XSL all you must do is add the xsl reference.

Here's the code:

```
$crlf = Chr(13) + Chr(10)

$tempstr
$Name
$Value
$v

$l = CreateObject("WbemScripting.SWbemLocator")
$svc = $l.ConnectServer(".", "root\cimv2")
$svc.Security_.AuthenticationLevel = 6
$svc.Security_.ImpersonationLevel = 3
$objs = $svc.InstancesOf("Win32_Process")

$ws = CreateObject("WScript.Shell")
$fso = CreateObject("Scripting.FileSystemObject")
$v=0

$txtstream = $fso.OpenTextFile($ws.CurrentDirectory + "\Win32_Process.xml", 2,
True, -2)
$txtstream.WriteLine("<?xml version='1.0' encoding='iso-8859-1'?>")
$txtstream.WriteLine("<?xml-stylesheet type='text/xsl' href=" + chr(34) +
$ws.CurrentDirectory + "\Win32_Process.xml" + Chr(34) + "?>")
$txtstream.WriteLine("<data>")

For Each $obj in $objs
   $txtstream.WriteLine("<win32_process>")
   For Each $prop in $obj.Properties_
```

```
        $txtstream.WriteLine("<" + $prop.Name + ">" + GetValue($prop.Name, $obj) +
"</" + $prop.Name + ">")
    Next
    $txtstream.WriteLine("</win32_process>")
Next
$txtstream.WriteLine("</data>")
$txtstream.Close

$cn = CreateObject("ADODB.Connection")
$cn.Open("Provider=MSXML2.DSOControl;")
$rs = CreateObject("ADODB.Recordset")

$rs.Open($ws.CurrentDirectory + "\Win32_Process.xml", $cn)
$rs.Save($ws.CurrentDirectory + "\Process_Schema.xml", 1)
```

Here's what's being created:


```
<?xml version='1.0' encoding='iso-8859-1'?>
<?xml-stylesheet type='text/xsl'
href="C:\Users\Administrator\Desktop\Win32_Process.xml"?>
<data>
<win32_process>
<Caption>System Idle Process</Caption>
<CommandLine></CommandLine>
<CreationClassName>Win32_Process</CreationClassName>
<CreationDate>04/04/2018 13:41:49</CreationDate>
<CSCreationClassName>Win32_ComputerSystem</CSCreationClassName>
<CSName>WIN-AH7FT1DMNVB</CSName>
<Description>System Idle Process</Description>
<ExecutablePath></ExecutablePath>
<ExecutionState></ExecutionState>
<Handle>0</Handle>
<HandleCount>0</HandleCount>
<InstallDate></InstallDate>
<KernelModeTime>5506987500000</KernelModeTime>
<MaximumWorkingSetSize></MaximumWorkingSetSize>
<MinimumWorkingSetSize></MinimumWorkingSetSize>
<Name>Win32_Process</Name>
<OSCreationClassName>Win32_OperatingSystem</OSCreationClassName>
```

<OSName>Microsoft Windows Server 2012 R2 Standard Evaluation|
C:\\Windows|\\Device\\Harddisk0\\Partition4</OSName>
<OtherOperationCount>0</OtherOperationCount>
<OtherTransferCount>0</OtherTransferCount>
<PageFaults>1</PageFaults>
<PageFileUsage>0</PageFileUsage>
<ParentProcessId>0</ParentProcessId>
<PeakPageFileUsage>0</PeakPageFileUsage>
<PeakVirtualSize>65536</PeakVirtualSize>
<PeakWorkingSetSize>4</PeakWorkingSetSize>
<Priority>0</Priority>
<PrivatePageCount>0</PrivatePageCount>
<ProcessId>0</ProcessId>
<QuotaNonPagedPoolUsage>0</QuotaNonPagedPoolUsage>
<QuotaPagedPoolUsage>0</QuotaPagedPoolUsage>
<QuotaPeakNonPagedPoolUsage>0</QuotaPeakNonPagedPoolUsage>
<QuotaPeakPagedPoolUsage>0</QuotaPeakPagedPoolUsage>
<ReadOperationCount>0</ReadOperationCount>
<ReadTransferCount>0</ReadTransferCount>
<SessionId>0</SessionId>
<Status></Status>
<TerminationDate></TerminationDate>
<ThreadCount>8</ThreadCount>
<UserModeTime>0</UserModeTime>
<VirtualSize>65536</VirtualSize>
<WindowsVersion>6.3.9600</WindowsVersion>
<WorkingSetSize>4</WorkingSetSize>
<WriteOperationCount>0</WriteOperationCount>
<WriteTransferCount>0</WriteTransferCount>
</win32_process>
<win32_process>

Schema XML

Basically, this code is combined with ADO to create a Schema file.

Below is the source code.

```
$crlf = Chr(13) + Chr(10)

$tempstr
$Name
$Value
$v

$l = CreateObject("WbemScripting.SWbemLocator")
$svc = $l.ConnectServer(".", "root\cimv2")
$svc.Security_.AuthenticationLevel = 6
$svc.Security_.ImpersonationLevel = 3
$objs = $svc.InstancesOf("Win32_Process")

$ws = CreateObject("WScript.Shell")
$fso = CreateObject("Scripting.FileSystemObject")
$v=0

$txtstream = $fso.OpenTextFile($ws.CurrentDirectory + "\Win32_Process.xml", 2,
True, -2)
$txtstream.WriteLine("<?xml version='1.0' encoding='iso-8859-1'?>")
$txtstream.WriteLine("<data>")

For Each $obj in $objs
  $txtstream.WriteLine("<win32_process>")
  For Each $prop in $obj.Properties_
    $txtstream.WriteLine("<" + $prop.Name + ">" + GetValue($prop.Name, $obj) +
"</" + $prop.Name + ">")
  Next
  $txtstream.WriteLine("</win32_process>")
Next
$txtstream.WriteLine("</data>")
```

```
$txtstream.Close

$cn = CreateObject("ADODB.Connection")
$cn.Open("Provider=MSDAOSP;Data Source=MSXML2.DSOControl;")
$rs = CreateObject("ADODB.Recordset")
$rs.Open($ws.CurrentDirectory + "\Win32_Process.xml", $cn)
$rs.Save($ws.CurrentDirectory + "\Process_Schema.xml", 1)
```

Below is a partial view of the schema File:


```
<?xml version='1.0'?>
- <xml xmlns:z='#RowsetSchema' xmlns:rs='urn:schemas-microsoft-com:rowset' xmlns:dt='uuid:C2F41010-65B3-11d1-A29F-00AA00C14882' xmlns:s='uuid:BDC6E3F0-6DA3-11d1-A2A3-00AA00C14882'>
  - <s:Schema id='RowsetSchema'>
    - <s:ElementType rs:BufferedUpd='false' rs:updatable='true' content='eltOnly' name='row'>
      + <s:AttributeType name='Caption' rs:write='true' rs:maydefer='true' rs:nullable='true' rs:number='1'>
      + <s:AttributeType name='CommandLine' rs:write='true' rs:maydefer='true' rs:nullable='true' rs:number='2'>
      + <s:AttributeType name='CreationClassName' rs:write='true' rs:maydefer='true' rs:nullable='true' rs:number='3'>
      + <s:AttributeType name='CreationDate' rs:write='true' rs:maydefer='true' rs:nullable='true' rs:number='4'>
      + <s:AttributeType name='CSCreationClassName' rs:write='true' rs:maydefer='true' rs:nullable='true' rs:number='5'>
      + <s:AttributeType name='CSName' rs:write='true' rs:maydefer='true' rs:nullable='true' rs:number='6'>
      + <s:AttributeType name='Description' rs:write='true' rs:maydefer='true' rs:nullable='true' rs:number='7'>
      + <s:AttributeType name='ExecutablePath' rs:write='true' rs:maydefer='true' rs:nullable='true' rs:number='8'>
      + <s:AttributeType name='ExecutionState' rs:write='true' rs:maydefer='true' rs:nullable='true' rs:number='9'>
      + <s:AttributeType name='Handle' rs:write='true' rs:maydefer='true' rs:nullable='true' rs:number='10'>
      + <s:AttributeType name='HandleCount' rs:write='true' rs:maydefer='true' rs:nullable='true' rs:number='11'>
      + <s:AttributeType name='InstallDate' rs:write='true' rs:maydefer='true' rs:nullable='true' rs:number='12'>
      + <s:AttributeType name='KernelModeTime' rs:write='true' rs:maydefer='true' rs:nullable='true' rs:number='13'>
      + <s:AttributeType name='MaximumWorkingSetSize' rs:write='true' rs:maydefer='true' rs:nullable='true' rs:number='14'>
      + <s:AttributeType name='MinimumWorkingSetSize' rs:write='true' rs:maydefer='true' rs:nullable='true' rs:number='15'>
      + <s:AttributeType name='Name' rs:write='true' rs:maydefer='true' rs:nullable='true' rs:number='16'>
      + <s:AttributeType name='OSCreationClassName' rs:write='true' rs:maydefer='true' rs:nullable='true' rs:number='17'>
      + <s:AttributeType name='OSName' rs:write='true' rs:maydefer='true' rs:nullable='true' rs:number='18'>
      + <s:AttributeType name='OtherOperationCount' rs:write='true' rs:maydefer='true' rs:nullable='true' rs:number='19'>
      + <s:AttributeType name='OtherTransferCount' rs:write='true' rs:maydefer='true' rs:nullable='true' rs:number='20'>
      + <s:AttributeType name='PageFaults' rs:write='true' rs:maydefer='true' rs:nullable='true' rs:number='21'>
      + <s:AttributeType name='PageFileUsage' rs:write='true' rs:maydefer='true' rs:nullable='true' rs:number='22'>
      + <s:AttributeType name='ParentProcessId' rs:write='true' rs:maydefer='true' rs:nullable='true' rs:number='23'>
      + <s:AttributeType name='PeakPageFileUsage' rs:write='true' rs:maydefer='true' rs:nullable='true' rs:number='24'>
      + <s:AttributeType name='PeakVirtualSize' rs:write='true' rs:maydefer='true' rs:nullable='true' rs:number='25'>
      + <s:AttributeType name='PeakWorkingSetSize' rs:write='true' rs:maydefer='true' rs:nullable='true' rs:number='26'>
      + <s:AttributeType name='Priority' rs:write='true' rs:maydefer='true' rs:nullable='true' rs:number='27'>
      + <s:AttributeType name='PrivatePageCount' rs:write='true' rs:maydefer='true' rs:nullable='true' rs:number='28'>
      + <s:AttributeType name='ProcessId' rs:write='true' rs:maydefer='true' rs:nullable='true' rs:number='29'>
      + <s:AttributeType name='QuotaNonPagedPoolUsage' rs:write='true' rs:maydefer='true' rs:nullable='true' rs:number='30'>
      + <s:AttributeType name='QuotaPagedPoolUsage' rs:write='true' rs:maydefer='true' rs:nullable='true' rs:number='31'>
      + <s:AttributeType name='QuotaPeakNonPagedPoolUsage' rs:write='true' rs:maydefer='true' rs:nullable='true' rs:number='32'>
      + <s:AttributeType name='QuotaPeakPagedPoolUsage' rs:write='true' rs:maydefer='true' rs:nullable='true' rs:number='33'>
      + <s:AttributeType name='ReadOperationCount' rs:write='true' rs:maydefer='true' rs:nullable='true' rs:number='34'>
      + <s:AttributeType name='ReadTransferCount' rs:write='true' rs:maydefer='true' rs:nullable='true' rs:number='35'>
      + <s:AttributeType name='SessionId' rs:write='true' rs:maydefer='true' rs:nullable='true' rs:number='36'>
      + <s:AttributeType name='Status' rs:write='true' rs:maydefer='true' rs:nullable='true' rs:number='37'>
      + <s:AttributeType name='TerminationDate' rs:write='true' rs:maydefer='true' rs:nullable='true' rs:number='38'>
      + <s:AttributeType name='ThreadCount' rs:write='true' rs:maydefer='true' rs:nullable='true' rs:number='39'>
      + <s:AttributeType name='UserModeTime' rs:write='true' rs:maydefer='true' rs:nullable='true' rs:number='40'>
      + <s:AttributeType name='VirtualSize' rs:write='true' rs:maydefer='true' rs:nullable='true' rs:number='41'>
      + <s:AttributeType name='WindowsVersion' rs:write='true' rs:maydefer='true' rs:nullable='true' rs:number='42'>
      + <s:AttributeType name='WorkingSetSize' rs:write='true' rs:maydefer='true' rs:nullable='true' rs:number='43'>
      + <s:AttributeType name='WriteOperationCount' rs:write='true' rs:maydefer='true' rs:nullable='true' rs:number='44'>
      + <s:AttributeType name='WriteTransferCount' rs:write='true' rs:maydefer='true' rs:nullable='true' rs:number='45'>
      + <s:AttributeType rs:name='$Text' name='c45' rs:write='true' rs:maydefer='true' rs:nullable='true' rs:number='46'>
        <s:extends type='rs:rowbase'/>
      </s:ElementType>
  </s:Schema>
```


And here's what it looks like in Excel:

A1 fx id

	A	B	C	D	E	F	G	H	I	J	K	L
1	id	name	content	ns3:updatable	ns3:BufferedUpd	name2	ns3:number	ns3:nullable	ns3:maydefer	ns3:write	ns3:name	ns1:type
2	RowsetSchema	row	eltOnly	TRUE	FALSE	Caption	1	TRUE	TRUE	TRUE		string
3	RowsetSchema	row	eltOnly	TRUE	FALSE	CommandLine	2	TRUE	TRUE	TRUE		string
4	RowsetSchema	row	eltOnly	TRUE	FALSE	CreationClassName	3	TRUE	TRUE	TRUE		string
5	RowsetSchema	row	eltOnly	TRUE	FALSE	CreationDate	4	TRUE	TRUE	TRUE		string
6	RowsetSchema	row	eltOnly	TRUE	FALSE	CSCreationClassName	5	TRUE	TRUE	TRUE		string
7	RowsetSchema	row	eltOnly	TRUE	FALSE	CSName	6	TRUE	TRUE	TRUE		string
8	RowsetSchema	row	eltOnly	TRUE	FALSE	Description	7	TRUE	TRUE	TRUE		string
9	RowsetSchema	row	eltOnly	TRUE	FALSE	ExecutablePath	8	TRUE	TRUE	TRUE		string
10	RowsetSchema	row	eltOnly	TRUE	FALSE	ExecutionState	9	TRUE	TRUE	TRUE		string
11	RowsetSchema	row	eltOnly	TRUE	FALSE	Handle	10	TRUE	TRUE	TRUE		string
12	RowsetSchema	row	eltOnly	TRUE	FALSE	HandleCount	11	TRUE	TRUE	TRUE		string
13	RowsetSchema	row	eltOnly	TRUE	FALSE	InstallDate	12	TRUE	TRUE	TRUE		string
14	RowsetSchema	row	eltOnly	TRUE	FALSE	KernelModeTime	13	TRUE	TRUE	TRUE		string
15	RowsetSchema	row	eltOnly	TRUE	FALSE	MaximumWorkingSetSize	14	TRUE	TRUE	TRUE		string
16	RowsetSchema	row	eltOnly	TRUE	FALSE	MinimumWorkingSetSize	15	TRUE	TRUE	TRUE		string
17	RowsetSchema	row	eltOnly	TRUE	FALSE	Name	16	TRUE	TRUE	TRUE		string
18	RowsetSchema	row	eltOnly	TRUE	FALSE	OSCreationClassName	17	TRUE	TRUE	TRUE		string
19	RowsetSchema	row	eltOnly	TRUE	FALSE	OSName	18	TRUE	TRUE	TRUE		string
20	RowsetSchema	row	eltOnly	TRUE	FALSE	OtherOperationCount	19	TRUE	TRUE	TRUE		string
21	RowsetSchema	row	eltOnly	TRUE	FALSE	OtherTransferCount	20	TRUE	TRUE	TRUE		string
22	RowsetSchema	row	eltOnly	TRUE	FALSE	PageFaults	21	TRUE	TRUE	TRUE		string
23	RowsetSchema	row	eltOnly	TRUE	FALSE	PageFileUsage	22	TRUE	TRUE	TRUE		string
24	RowsetSchema	row	eltOnly	TRUE	FALSE	ParentProcessId	23	TRUE	TRUE	TRUE		string
25	RowsetSchema	row	eltOnly	TRUE	FALSE	PeakPageFileUsage	24	TRUE	TRUE	TRUE		string
26	RowsetSchema	row	eltOnly	TRUE	FALSE	PeakVirtualSize	25	TRUE	TRUE	TRUE		string
27	RowsetSchema	row	eltOnly	TRUE	FALSE	PeakWorkingSetSize	26	TRUE	TRUE	TRUE		string
28	RowsetSchema	row	eltOnly	TRUE	FALSE	Priority	27	TRUE	TRUE	TRUE		string
29	RowsetSchema	row	eltOnly	TRUE	FALSE	PrivatePageCount	28	TRUE	TRUE	TRUE		string
30	RowsetSchema	row	eltOnly	TRUE	FALSE	ProcessId	29	TRUE	TRUE	TRUE		string
31	RowsetSchema	row	eltOnly	TRUE	FALSE	QuotaNonPagedPoolUsage	30	TRUE	TRUE	TRUE		string
32	RowsetSchema	row	eltOnly	TRUE	FALSE	QuotaPagedPoolUsage	31	TRUE	TRUE	TRUE		string
33	RowsetSchema	row	eltOnly	TRUE	FALSE	QuotaPeakNonPagedPoolUsage	32	TRUE	TRUE	TRUE		string
34	RowsetSchema	row	eltOnly	TRUE	FALSE	QuotaPeakPagedPoolUsage	33	TRUE	TRUE	TRUE		string
35	RowsetSchema	row	eltOnly	TRUE	FALSE	ReadOperationCount	34	TRUE	TRUE	TRUE		string

Creating reports from the output files

Okay, so we created this xml, let's make some reports from it.

Element xml

```
$cn = CreateObject("ADODB.Connection")
$cn.Open("Provider=MSXML2.DSOControl;")
$rs = CreateObject("ADODB.Recordset")
$rs.Open($ws.CurrentDirectory + "\Win32_Process.xml", $cn)
$ws = CreateObject("WScript.Shell")
$fso = CreateObject("Scripting.FileSystemObject")
$txtstream = $fso.OpenTextFile("C:\Process.html", 2, true, -2)
$txtstream.WriteLine("<html>")
$txtstream.WriteLine("<head>")
$txtstream.WriteLine("<title>Products</title>")
$txtstream.WriteLine("</head>")
$txtstream.WriteLine("<body bgcolor=#333333>")
$txtstream.WriteLine("<center>")
$txtstream.WriteLine("<table colspacing=3 colpadding=3>")
$txtstream.WriteLine("<tr>")
$count = $rs.Fields.Count -1
for $x = 0 To $count
   $txtstream.WriteLine("<th>" + $rs.Fields($x).Name  + "</th>")
Next
```

```
$txtstream.WriteLine("</tr>")

$rs.MoveLast()
$rs.MoveFirst()

while($rs.eof = false)

   $txtstream.WriteLine("<tr>")
   for $x=0 To $Count
      $txtstream.WriteLine("<td>" + $rs.Fields($x).Value  + "</td>")
   Next
   $txtstream.WriteLine("</tr>")
   $rs.MoveNext()

Loop
$txtstream.WriteLine("</table>")
$txtstream.WriteLine("</html>")
$txtstream.close
```

Here's the html View:

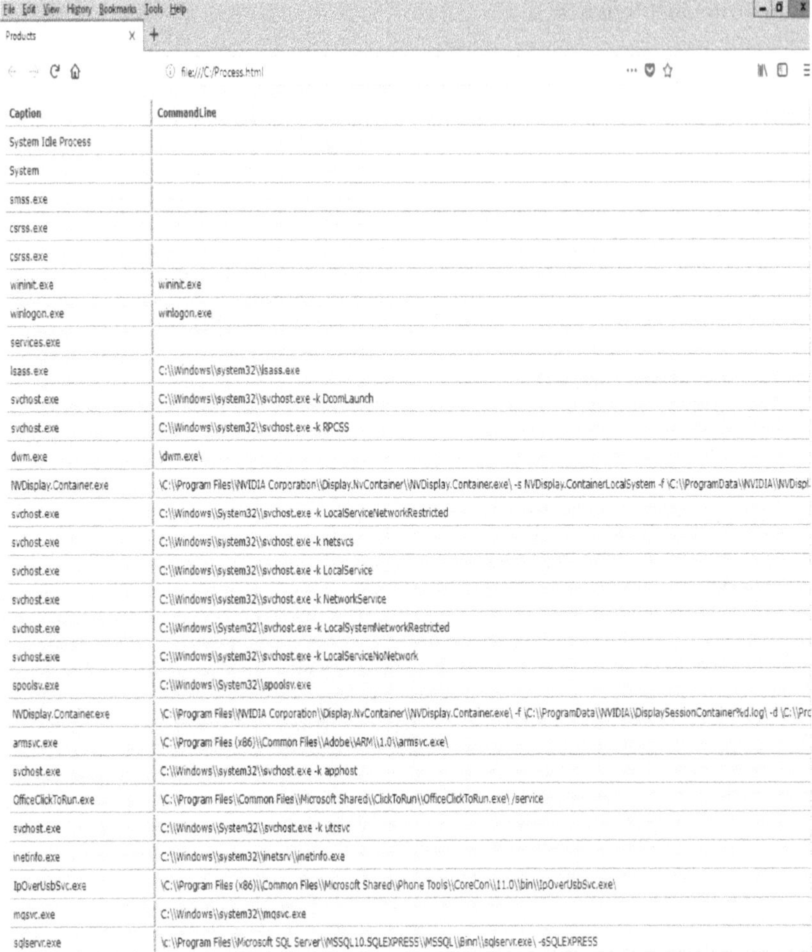

Caption	CommandLine
System Idle Process	
System	
smss.exe	
csrss.exe	
csrss.exe	
wininit.exe	wininit.exe
winlogon.exe	winlogon.exe
services.exe	
lsass.exe	C:\\Windows\\system32\\lsass.exe
svchost.exe	C:\\Windows\\system32\\svchost.exe -k DcomLaunch
svchost.exe	C:\\Windows\\system32\\svchost.exe -k RPCSS
dwm.exe	\dwm.exe\
NVDisplay.Container.exe	\C:\\Program Files\\NVIDIA Corporation\\Display.NvContainer\\NVDisplay.Container.exe\ -s NVDisplay.ContainerLocalSystem -f \C:\\ProgramData\\NVIDIA\\NVDispl
svchost.exe	C:\\Windows\\System32\\svchost.exe -k LocalServiceNetworkRestricted
svchost.exe	C:\\Windows\\system32\\svchost.exe -k netsvcs
svchost.exe	C:\\Windows\\system32\\svchost.exe -k LocalService
svchost.exe	C:\\Windows\\system32\\svchost.exe -k NetworkService
svchost.exe	C:\\Windows\\System32\\svchost.exe -k LocalSystemNetworkRestricted
svchost.exe	C:\\Windows\\system32\\svchost.exe -k LocalServiceNoNetwork
spoolsv.exe	C:\\Windows\\System32\\spoolsv.exe
NVDisplay.Container.exe	\C:\\Program Files\\NVIDIA Corporation\\Display.NvContainer\\NVDisplay.Container.exe\ -f \C:\\ProgramData\\NVIDIA\\DisplaySessionContainer%d.log\ -d \C:\\Pro
armsvc.exe	\C:\\Program Files (x86)\\Common Files\\Adobe\\ARM\\1.0\\armsvc.exe\
svchost.exe	C:\\Windows\\system32\\svchost.exe -k apphost
OfficeClickToRun.exe	\C:\\Program Files\\Common Files\\Microsoft Shared\\ClickToRun\\OfficeClickToRun.exe\ /service
svchost.exe	C:\\Windows\\System32\\svchost.exe -k utcsvc
inetinfo.exe	C:\\Windows\\system32\\inetsrv\\inetinfo.exe
IpOverUsbSvc.exe	\C:\\Program Files (x86)\\Common Files\\Microsoft Shared\\Phone Tools\\CoreCon\\11.0\\bin\\IpOverUsbSvc.exe\
mqsvc.exe	C:\\Windows\\system32\\mqsvc.exe
sqlservr.exe	\c:\\Program Files\\Microsoft SQL Server\\MSSQL10.SQLEXPRESS\\MSSQL\\Binn\\sqlservr.exe\ -sSQLEXPRESS

But here's the issue. We're using ADO. Why not go native?

```
$xmlDoc = CreateObject("MSXML2.DOMDocument")
$xmlDoc.Load("C:\Win32_Process.xml")
$nl = $xmlDoc.GetElementsByTagName("win32_process")

$ws = CreateObject("WScript.Shell")
```

```
$fso = CreateObject("Scripting.FileSystemObject")
$txtstream = $fso.OpenTextFile("C:\Process.html", 2, true, -2)
$txtstream.WriteLine("<html>")
$txtstream.WriteLine("<head>")
$txtstream.WriteLine("<title>Products</title>")
$txtstream.WriteLine("</head>")
$txtstream.WriteLine("<body bgcolor=#333333>")
$txtstream.WriteLine("<center>")
$txtstream.WriteLine("<table colspacing=3 colpadding=3>")
$txtstream.WriteLine("<tr>")
$nl1 = $nl.Item(0)
For each $cNode in $nl1.ChildNodes
   $txtstream.WriteLine("<th>" + $cNode.NodeName + "</th>")
Next
$txtstream.WriteLine("</tr>")
For each $nl1 in $nl
   $txtstream.WriteLine("<tr>")
   For each $cNode in $nl1.ChildNodes
      $txtstream.WriteLine("<td>" + $cNode.Text  + "</td>")
   Next
   $txtstream.WriteLine("</tr>")
Next
$txtstream.WriteLine("</table>")
$txtstream.WriteLine("</html>")
$txtstream.close
```

And, of course, here's the output:

Caption	CommandLine
System Idle Process	
System	
smss.exe	
csrss.exe	
csrss.exe	
wininit.exe	wininit.exe
winlogon.exe	winlogon.exe
services.exe	
lsass.exe	C:\\Windows\\system32\\lsass.exe
svchost.exe	C:\\Windows\\system32\\svchost.exe -k DcomLaunch
svchost.exe	C:\\Windows\\system32\\svchost.exe -k RPCSS
dwm.exe	\dwm.exe\
NVDisplay.Container.exe	\C:\\Program Files\\NVIDIA Corporation\\Display.NvContainer\\NVDisplay.Container.exe\ -s NVDisplay.ContainerLocalSystem -f \C:\\ProgramData\\NVIDIA\\NVDisplay.ContainerLocalSystem.log\ -l 3 -d \C:\\Program Files\\NVIDIA Corpora
svchost.exe	C:\\Windows\\System32\\svchost.exe -k LocalServiceNetworkRestricted
svchost.exe	C:\\Windows\\system32\\svchost.exe -k netsvcs
svchost.exe	C:\\Windows\\system32\\svchost.exe -k LocalService
svchost.exe	C:\\Windows\\system32\\svchost.exe -k NetworkService
svchost.exe	C:\\Windows\\System32\\svchost.exe -k LocalSystemNetworkRestricted
svchost.exe	C:\\Windows\\system32\\svchost.exe -k LocalServiceNoNetwork
spoolsv.exe	C:\\Windows\\System32\\spoolsv.exe
NVDisplay.Container.exe	\C:\\Program Files\\NVIDIA Corporation\\Display.NvContainer\\NVDisplay.Container.exe\ -f \C:\\ProgramData\\NVIDIA\\DisplaySessionContainer%d.log\ -d \C:\\Program Files\\NVIDIA Corporation\\Display.NvContainer\\plugins\\Session\
armsvc.exe	\C:\\Program Files (x86)\\Common Files\\Adobe\\ARM\\1.0\\armsvc.exe\
svchost.exe	C:\\Windows\\system32\\svchost.exe -k apphost
OfficeClickToRun.exe	\C:\\Program Files\\Common Files\\Microsoft Shared\\ClickToRun\\OfficeClickToRun.exe\ /service
svchost.exe	C:\\Windows\\System32\\svchost.exe -k utcsvc
inetinfo.exe	C:\\Windows\\system32\\inetsrv\\inetinfo.exe
IpOverUsbSvc.exe	\C:\\Program Files (x86)\\Common Files\\Microsoft Shared\\Phone Tools\\CoreCon\\11.0\\bin\\IpOverUsbSvc.exe\
mqsvc.exe	C:\\Windows\\system32\\mqsvc.exe
sqlservr.exe	\c:\\Program Files\\Microsoft SQL Server\\MSSQL10.SQLEXPRESS\\MSSQL\\Binn\\sqlservr.exe\ -sSQLEXPRESS
SMSvcHost.exe	C:\\Windows\\Microsoft.NET\\Framework64\\v4.0.30319\\SMSvcHost.exe
nvcontainer.exe	\C:\\Program Files\\NVIDIA Corporation\\NvContainer\\nvcontainer.exe\ -s NvContainerLocalSystem -a -f \C:\\ProgramData\\NVIDIA\\NvContainerLocalSystem.log\ -l 3 -d \C:\\Program Files\\NVIDIA Corporation\\NvContainer\\plugins\\L
NvTelemetryContainer.exe	\C:\\Program Files (x86)\\NVIDIA Corporation\\NvTelemetry\\NvTelemetryContainer.exe\ -s NvTelemetryContainer -f \C:\\ProgramData\\NVIDIA\\NvTelemetryContainer.log\ -l 3 -d \C:\\Program Files (x86)\\NVIDIA Corporation\\NvTelem
sqlwriter.exe	\c:\\Program Files\\Microsoft SQL Server\\90\\Shared\\sqlwriter.exe\
svchost.exe	C:\\Windows\\system32\\svchost.exe -k imgsvc
TeamViewer_Service.exe	\C:\\Program Files (x86)\\TeamViewer\\TeamViewer_Service.exe\
svchost.exe	C:\\Windows\\system32\\svchost.exe -k iissvcs
wlms.exe	C:\\Windows\\system32\\wlms\\wlms.exe
mqtgsvc.exe	C:\\Windows\\system32\\mqtgsvc.exe
SMSvcHost.exe	\C:\\Windows\\Microsoft.NET\\Framework64\\v4.0.30319\\SMSvcHost.exe\ -NetMsmqActivator

Attribute XML rendering

To the best of my knowledge, there isn't a provider that can deal with Attribute xml. So, we'll use MSXML once again to help us render it.

```
$xmlDoc = CreateObject("MSXML2.DOMDocument")
$xmlDoc.Load("C:\Win32_Process.xml")
$nl = $xmlDoc.GetElementsByTagName("win32_process")

$ws = CreateObject("WScript.Shell")
$fso = CreateObject("Scripting.FileSystemObject")
$txtstream = $fso.OpenTextFile("C:\Process.html", 2, true, -2)
$txtstream.WriteLine("<html>")
$txtstream.WriteLine("<head>")
$txtstream.WriteLine("<title>Products</title>")
$txtstream.WriteLine("</head>")
$txtstream.WriteLine("<body bgcolor=#333333>")
$txtstream.WriteLine("<center>")

For Each $nl1 in $nl
  $txtstream.WriteLine("<table colspacing=3 colpadding=3>")
  $txtstream.WriteLine("<tr>")
  $cNode1 = $nl1.ChildNodes.Item(0)
  $txtstream.WriteLine("<tr>")
  For Each $at in $cNode1.Attributes
    $txtstream.WriteLine("<th>" + $at.NodeName + "</th>")
  Next
  $txtstream.WriteLine("</tr>")
  For Each $cNode in $nl1.ChildNodes
      $txtstream.WriteLine("<tr>")
      $atts = $cNode.Attributes
      For Each $att in $atts
         $txtstream.WriteLine("<td>" + $att.Value  + "</td>")
      Next
      $txtstream.WriteLine("</tr>")
  Next
```

```
  $txtstream.WriteLine("</table>")
  $txtstream.WriteLine("</br>")
Next
$txtstream.WriteLine("</body>")
$txtstream.WriteLine("</html>")
$txtstream.close
```

And this is what it looks like:

name	datatype	controltype	value
Caption	string	Textbox	System Idle Process
CommandLine	string	Textbox	
CreationClassName	string	Textbox	Win32_Process
CreationDate	string	Textbox	04/04/2018 13:41:49
CSCreationClassName	string	Textbox	Win32_ComputerSystem
CSName	string	Textbox	WIN-AM7FT1DMNVB
Description	string	Textbox	System Idle Process
ExecutablePath	string	Textbox	
ExecutionState	string	Textbox	
Handle	string	Textbox	0
HandleCount	string	Textbox	0
InstallDate	string	Textbox	
KernelModeTime	string	Textbox	6600240468790
MaximumWorkingSetSize	string	Textbox	
MinimumWorkingSetSize	string	Textbox	
Name	string	Textbox	Win32_Process
OSCreationClassName	string	Textbox	Win32_OperatingSystem
OSName	string	Textbox	Microsoft Windows Server 2012 R2 Standard Evaluation|C:\\Windows|\\Device\\Harddisk0\\Partition4
OtherOperationCount	string	Textbox	0
OtherTransferCount	string	Textbox	0
PageFaults	string	Textbox	1
PageFileUsage	string	Textbox	0
ParentProcessId	string	Textbox	0
PeakPageFileUsage	string	Textbox	0
PeakVirtualSize	string	Textbox	65536
PeakWorkingSetSize	string	Textbox	4
Priority	string	Textbox	0
PrivatePageCount	string	Textbox	0
ProcessId	string	Textbox	0
QuotaNonPagedPoolUsage	string	Textbox	0
QuotaPagedPoolUsage	string	Textbox	0
QuotaPeakNonPagedPoolUsage	string	Textbox	0
QuotaPeakPagedPoolUsage	string	Textbox	0
ReadOperationCount	string	Textbox	0
ReadTransferCount	string	Textbox	0
SessionId	string	Textbox	0
Status	string	Textbox	
TerminationDate	string	Textbox	
ThreadCount	string	Textbox	8
UserModeTime	string	Textbox	0
VirtualSize	string	Textbox	65536
WindowsVersion	string	Textbox	6.3.9600
WorkingSetSize	string	Textbox	4
WriteOperationCount	string	Textbox	0
WriteTransferCount	string	Textbox	0

SCHEMA XML

Like Element xml there is a provider and MSXML that can help you render the xml.

Provider:

```
$cn = CreateObject("ADODB.Connection")
$rs = CreateObject("ADODB.Recordset")

$cn.Open("Provider=MSPersist")
```

```
$rs = CreateObject("ADODB.Recordset")
$rs.Open("C:\Schema.xml", $cn,,,256)

$ws = CreateObject("WScript.Shell")
$fso = CreateObject("Scripting.FileSystemObject")
$txtstream = $fso.OpenTextFile("C:\Process.html", 2, true, -2)
$txtstream.WriteLine("<html>")
$txtstream.WriteLine("<head>")
$txtstream.WriteLine("<title>Products</title>")
$txtstream.WriteLine("</head>")
$txtstream.WriteLine("<body bgcolor=#333333>")
$txtstream.WriteLine("<center>")
$txtstream.WriteLine("<table colspacing=3 colpadding=3>")
$txtstream.WriteLine("<tr>")
$count = $rs.Fields.Count -2
for $x = 0 To $count
   $txtstream.WriteLine("<th>" + $rs.Fields($x).Name  + "</th>")
Next
$txtstream.WriteLine("</tr>")

$rs.MoveLast()
$rs.MoveFirst()

while($rs.eof = false)

   $txtstream.WriteLine("<tr>")
   for $x=0 To $Count
      $txtstream.WriteLine("<td>" + $rs.Fields($x).Value  + "</td>")
   Next
   $txtstream.WriteLine("</tr>")
   $rs.MoveNext()
Loop
$txtstream.WriteLine("</table>")
$txtstream.WriteLine("</html>")
$txtstream.close
```

Here's the html View:

Caption	CommandLine
System Idle Process	
System	
smss.exe	
csrss.exe	
csrss.exe	
wininit.exe	wininit.exe
winlogon.exe	winlogon.exe
services.exe	
lsass.exe	C:\\Windows\\system32\\lsass.exe
svchost.exe	C:\\Windows\\system32\\svchost.exe -k DcomLaunch
svchost.exe	C:\\Windows\\system32\\svchost.exe -k RPCSS
dwm.exe	\dwm.exe\
NVDisplay.Container.exe	\C:\\Program Files\\NVIDIA Corporation\\Display.NvContainer\\NVDisplay.Container.exe\ -s NVDisplay.ContainerLocalSystem -f \C:\\ProgramData\\NVIDIA\\NVDisplay.ContainerLocalSystem.log\ -l 3 -d \C:\\Program Files\\NVIDIA Corporation\\Display.NvContainer\\plugin
svchost.exe	C:\\Windows\\System32\\svchost.exe -k LocalServiceNetworkRestricted
svchost.exe	C:\\Windows\\system32\\svchost.exe -k netsvcs
svchost.exe	C:\\Windows\\system32\\svchost.exe -k LocalService
svchost.exe	C:\\Windows\\system32\\svchost.exe -k NetworkService
svchost.exe	C:\\Windows\\System32\\svchost.exe -k LocalSystemNetworkRestricted
svchost.exe	C:\\Windows\\system32\\svchost.exe -k LocalServiceNoNetwork
spoolsv.exe	C:\\Windows\\System32\\spoolsv.exe
NVDisplay.Container.exe	\C:\\Program Files\\NVIDIA Corporation\\Display.NvContainer\\NVDisplay.Container.exe\ -f \C:\\ProgramData\\NVIDIA\\DisplaySessionContainer%d.log\ -d \C:\\Program Files\\NVIDIA Corporation\\Display.NvContainer\\plugins\\Session\ -r -l 3 -p 30000 -c
armsvc.exe	\C:\\Program Files (x86)\\Common Files\\Adobe\\ARM\\1.0\\armsvc.exe\
svchost.exe	C:\\Windows\\system32\\svchost.exe -k apphost
OfficeClickToRun.exe	\C:\\Program Files\\Common Files\\Microsoft Shared\\ClickToRun\\OfficeClickToRun.exe\ /service
svchost.exe	C:\\Windows\\System32\\svchost.exe -k utcsvc
inetinfo.exe	C:\\Windows\\system32\\inetsrv\\inetinfo.exe
IpOverUsbSvc.exe	\C:\\Program Files (x86)\\Common Files\\Microsoft Shared\\Phone Tools\\CoreCon\\11.0\\bin\\IpOverUsbSvc.exe\
mqsvc.exe	C:\\Windows\\system32\\mqsvc.exe
sqlservr.exe	\c:\\Program Files\\Microsoft SQL Server\\MSSQL10.SQLEXPRESS\\MSSQL\\Binn\\sqlservr.exe\ -sSQLEXPRESS
SMSvcHost.exe	C:\\Windows\\Microsoft.NET\\Framework64\\v4.0.30319\\SMSvcHost.exe
nvcontainer.exe	\C:\\Program Files\\NVIDIA Corporation\\NvContainer\\nvcontainer.exe\ -s NvContainerLocalSystem -a -f \C:\\ProgramData\\NVIDIA\\NvContainerLocalSystem.log\ -l 3 -d \C:\\Program Files\\NVIDIA Corporation\\NvContainer\\plugins\\LocalSystem\ -r -p 30000 -st \C:
NvTelemetryContainer.exe	\C:\\Program Files (x86)\\NVIDIA Corporation\\NvTelemetry\\NvTelemetryContainer.exe\ -s NvTelemetryContainer -f \C:\\ProgramData\\NVIDIA\\NvTelemetryContainer.log\ -l 3 -d \C:\\Program Files (x86)\\NVIDIA Corporation\\NvTelemetry\\plugins\ -r
sqlwriter.exe	\c:\\Program Files\\Microsoft SQL Server\\90\\Shared\\sqlwriter.exe\
svchost.exe	C:\\Windows\\system32\\svchost.exe -k imgsvc
TeamViewer_Service.exe	\C:\\Program Files (x86)\\TeamViewer\\TeamViewer_Service.exe\
svchost.exe	C:\\Windows\\system32\\svchost.exe -k iissvcs
wlms.exe	C:\\Windows\\system32\\wlms\\wlms.exe
mqtgsvc.exe	C:\\Windows\\system32\\mqtgsvc.exe
SMSvcHost.exe	\C:\\Windows\\Microsoft.NET\\Framework64\\v4.0.30319\\SMSvcHost.exe\ -NetMsmqActivator
vmms.exe	C:\\Windows\\system32\\vmms.exe
BuildService.exe	\C:\\Program Files (x86)\\Xoreax\\IncrediBuild\\BuildService.exe\
CoordService.exe	\C:\\Program Files (x86)\\Xoreax\\IncrediBuild\\CoordService.exe\
svchost.exe	C:\\Windows\\System32\\svchost.exe -k termsvcs
svchost.exe	C:\\Windows\\system32\\svchost.exe -k NetworkServiceNetworkRestricted

If you think I'm using the same image repeatedly, take a good look at the code, there is a -2 on the count. That's because the last field is a collection of all the fields. And since that would make the report ugly, I've removed the field.

Now for the MSXML rendering.

```
$xmlDoc = CreateObject("MSXML2.DOMDocument")
$xmlDoc.Load("C:\Win32_Process.xml")
$nl = $xmlDoc.GetElementsByTagName("z:row")

$ws = CreateObject("WScript.Shell")
```

```
$fso = CreateObject("Scripting.FileSystemObject")
$txtstream = $fso.OpenTextFile("C:\Process.html", 2, true, -2)
$txtstream.WriteLine("<html>")
$txtstream.WriteLine("<head>")
$txtstream.WriteLine("<title>Products</title>")
$txtstream.WriteLine("</head>")
$txtstream.WriteLine("<body bgcolor=#333333>")
$txtstream.WriteLine("<center>")
$txtstream.WriteLine("<table colspacing=3 colpadding=3>")
$txtstream.WriteLine("<tr>")
$nl1 = $nl.Item(0)
For each $aNode in $nl1.Attributes
   $txtstream.WriteLine("<th>" + $aNode.NodeName + "</th>")
Next
$txtstream.WriteLine("</tr>")
For each $nl1 in $nl
   $txtstream.WriteLine("<tr>")
   For each $aNode in $nl1.Attributes
      $txtstream.WriteLine("<td>" + $aNode.Value  + "</td>")
   Next
   $txtstream.WriteLine("</tr>")
Next
$txtstream.WriteLine("</table>")
$txtstream.WriteLine("</html>")
$txtstream.close
```

A view of the output.

Caption	CommandLine
System Idle Process	
System	
smss.exe	
csrss.exe	
csrss.exe	
wininit.exe	wininit.exe
winlogon.exe	winlogon.exe
services.exe	
lsass.exe	C:\Windows\system32\lsass.exe
svchost.exe	C:\Windows\system32\svchost.exe -k DcomLaunch
svchost.exe	C:\Windows\system32\svchost.exe -k RPCSS
dwm.exe	"dwm.exe"
NVDisplay.Container.exe	"C:\Program Files\NVIDIA Corporation\Display.NvContainer\NVDisplay.Container.exe" -s NVDisplay.ContainerLocalSystem -f "C:\ProgramData\NVIDIA\NVDisplay.ContainerLocalSystem.log" -l 3 -d "C:\Program Files\NVIDIA Corporation\Display.NvContainer\plugin
svchost.exe	C:\Windows\System32\svchost.exe -k LocalServiceNetworkRestricted
svchost.exe	C:\Windows\system32\svchost.exe -k netsvcs
svchost.exe	C:\Windows\system32\svchost.exe -k LocalService
svchost.exe	C:\Windows\system32\svchost.exe -k NetworkService
svchost.exe	C:\Windows\System32\svchost.exe -k LocalSystemNetworkRestricted
svchost.exe	C:\Windows\system32\svchost.exe -k LocalServiceNoNetwork
spoolsv.exe	C:\Windows\System32\spoolsv.exe
NVDisplay.Container.exe	"C:\Program Files\NVIDIA Corporation\Display.NvContainer\NVDisplay.Container.exe" -f "C:\ProgramData\NVIDIA\DisplaySessionContainer%d.log" -d "C:\Program Files\NVIDIA Corporation\Display.NvContainer\plugins\Session" -r -l 3 -p 30000 -c
armsvc.exe	"C:\Program Files (x86)\Common Files\Adobe\ARM\1.0\armsvc.exe"
svchost.exe	C:\Windows\system32\svchost.exe -k apphost
OfficeClickToRun.exe	"C:\Program Files\Common Files\Microsoft Shared\ClickToRun\OfficeClickToRun.exe" /service
svchost.exe	C:\Windows\System32\svchost.exe -k utcsvc
inetinfo.exe	C:\Windows\system32\inetsrv\inetinfo.exe
IpOverUsbSvc.exe	"C:\Program Files (x86)\Common Files\Microsoft Shared\Phone Tools\CoreCon\11.0\bin\IpOverUsbSvc.exe"
mqsvc.exe	C:\Windows\system32\mqsvc.exe
sqlservr.exe	"c:\Program Files\Microsoft SQL Server\MSSQL10.SQLEXPRESS\MSSQL\Binn\sqlservr.exe" -sSQLEXPRESS
SMSvcHost.exe	C:\Windows\Microsoft.NET\Framework64\v4.0.30319\SMSvcHost.exe
nvcontainer.exe	"C:\Program Files\NVIDIA Corporation\NvContainer\nvcontainer.exe" -s NvContainerLocalSystem -a -f "C:\ProgramData\NVIDIA\NvContainerLocalSystem.log" -l 3 -d "C:\Program Files\NVIDIA Corporation\NvContainer\plugins\LocalSystem" -r -p 30000 -st "C.
NvTelemetryContainer.exe	"C:\Program Files (x86)\NVIDIA Corporation\NvTelemetry\NvTelemetryContainer.exe" -s NvTelemetryContainer -f "C:\ProgramData\NVIDIA\NvTelemetryContainer.log" -l 3 -d "C:\Program Files (x86)\NVIDIA Corporation\NvTelemetry\plugins" -r
sqlwriter.exe	"c:\Program Files\Microsoft SQL Server\90\Shared\sqlwriter.exe"
svchost.exe	C:\Windows\system32\svchost.exe -k imgsvc
TeamViewer_Service.exe	"C:\Program Files (x86)\TeamViewer\TeamViewer_Service.exe"
svchost.exe	C:\Windows\system32\svchost.exe -k iissvcs
wlms.exe	C:\Windows\system32\wlms\wlms.exe
mqtgsvc.exe	C:\Windows\system32\mqtgsvc.exe
SMSvcHost.exe	"C:\Windows\Microsoft.NET\Framework64\v4.0.30319\SMSvcHost.exe" -NetMsmqActivator
vmms.exe	C:\Windows\system32\vmms.exe
BuildService.exe	"C:\Program Files (x86)\Xoreax\IncrediBuild\BuildService.exe"
CoordService.exe	"C:\Program Files (x86)\Xoreax\IncrediBuild\CoordService.exe"
svchost.exe	C:\Windows\System32\svchost.exe -k termsvcs
svchost.exe	C:\Windows\system32\svchost.exe -k NetworkServiceNetworkRestricted

Stuff you will want to know

Below, is some information that might prove helpful.

Evaluators Or ways to compare things

There are ways in which you can compare things. These, in VB are the following:
== equals
< less than
> greater than
<> not equal to
<= equal to and less than
=> equal to and greater than

Something to do just for fun

Open Notepad and type this:

```
'Just another way to let your users know something has happened.
$ws = CreateObject("WScript.Shell")
$ws.Run("Https://www.Bing.com")
$ws.Run("Https://www.Facebook.com")
$ws.Run("Https://www.Google.com")
```

```
$ws.Run("Https://www.Yahoo.com")
```

Save the file as "FavoriteSites.kix". Once the file is created, double click on it. Whatever your default browser is, it should come up and display all the sites each in a separate tab.

Working With XSL

Well, we're getting near the end of this e-book. By now, you're probably looking at a lot of code wondering, will all this work?
I can assure you that its working for me. Of course, that presumes you have the latest build of Kixtart and you have Office 365 installed.
Beyond that and with other variables which could cause you to have issues, I can't assure you that any of this will work for you.
But it did work for me.
With that said, let's work on some XSL can be used – with respect to data mining – four different ways using element xml as its data source:

1. Single Line Horizontal
2. Multi Line Horizontal
3. Single Line Vertical
4. Multi line Vertical

I'm going to show you these first and then we're going to add some controls to each one.

The XML that will be rendered

Below is the xml that is going to be used for rendering:

```
$crlf = Chr(13) + Chr(10)

$tempstr
```

```
$Name
$Value
$v

$l = CreateObject("WbemScripting.SWbemLocator")
$svc = $l.ConnectServer(".", "root\cimv2")
$svc.Security_.AuthenticationLevel = 6
$svc.Security_.ImpersonationLevel = 3
$objs = $svc.InstancesOf("Win32_Process")

$ws = CreateObject("WScript.Shell")
$fso = CreateObject("Scripting.FileSystemObject")
$v=0

$txtstream = $fso.OpenTextFile($ws.CurrentDirectory + "\Win32_Process.xml", 2,
True, -2)
$txtstream.WriteLine("<?xml version=" + chr(34) + "1.0" + chr(34) + " encoding="
+ chr(34) + "iso-8859-1" + chr(34) + "?>")
$txtstream.WriteLine("<?xml-stylesheet type=" + chr(34) + "text/xsl" + chr(34) + "
href=" + chr(34) + "Process.xsl" + chr(34) + "?>")
$txtstream.WriteLine("<data>")

For Each $obj in $objs
   $txtstream.WriteLine("<win32_process>")
   For Each $prop in $obj.Properties_
      $txtstream.WriteLine("<" + $prop.Name + ">" + GetValue($prop.Name, $obj) +
"</" + $prop.Name + ">")
   Next
   $txtstream.WriteLine("</win32_process>")
Next
$txtstream.WriteLine("</data>")
$txtstream.Close

$cn = CreateObject("ADODB.Connection")
$cn.Open("Provider=MSXML2.DSOControl;")
$rs = CreateObject("ADODB.Recordset")
$rs.Open($ws.CurrentDirectory + "\Win32_Process.xml", $cn)
$rs.Save($ws.CurrentDirectory + "\Process_Schema.xml", 1)
```

Single Line Horizontal

Here's the single line horizontal xsl code:

```
$l = CreateObject("WbemScripting.SWbemLocator")
$svc = $l.ConnectServer(".", "root\cimv2")
$svc.Security_.AuthenticationLevel = 6
$svc.Security_.ImpersonationLevel = 3
$objs = $svc.InstancesOf("Win32_Process")


$ws = CreateObject("WScript.Shell")
$fso = CreateObject("Scripting.FileSystemObject")
$txtstream = $fso.OpenTextFile($ws.CurrentDirectory + "\Process.xsl", 2, true, -2)
$txtstream.WriteLine("<?xml version=" + chr(34) + "1.0" + chr(34) + " encoding="
+ chr(34) + "UTF-8" + chr(34) + "?>")
$txtstream.WriteLine("<xsl:stylesheet version=" + chr(34) + "1.0" + chr(34) + "
xmlns:xsl=" + chr(34) + "http://www.w3.org/1999/XSL/Transform" + chr(34) + ">")
$txtstream.WriteLine("<xsl:template match=" + chr(34) + "/" + chr(34) + ">")
$txtstream.WriteLine("<html>")
$txtstream.WriteLine("<head>")
$txtstream.WriteLine("<title>Products</title>")
$txtstream.WriteLine("</head>")
$txtstream.WriteLine("<body bgcolor=" + chr(34) + "#333333" + chr(34) + ">")
$txtstream.WriteLine("<table colspacing=" + chr(34) + "3" + chr(34) + "
colpadding=" + chr(34) + "3" + chr(34) + ">")
$obj = $objs.ItemIndex(0)
$txtstream.writeline("<tr>")
For Each $prop In $obj.Properties_
   $txtstream.writeline("<th align='left' nowrap='true'>" + $prop.Name + "</th>")
Next
$txtstream.writeline("</tr>")
$txtstream.writeline("<tr>")
For Each $prop In $obj.Properties_
   $txtstream.writeline("<td align='left' nowrap='true'><xsl:value-of select=" +
chr(34) + "data/win32_process/" + $prop.Name + chr(34) + "/></td>")
Next
$txtstream.writeline("</tr>")
$txtstream.WriteLine("</table>")
```

```
$txtstream.WriteLine("</body>")
$txtstream.WriteLine("</html>")
$txtstream.WriteLine("</xsl:template>")
$txtstream.WriteLine("</xsl:stylesheet>")
$txtstream.Close()
```

Here's what it looks like:

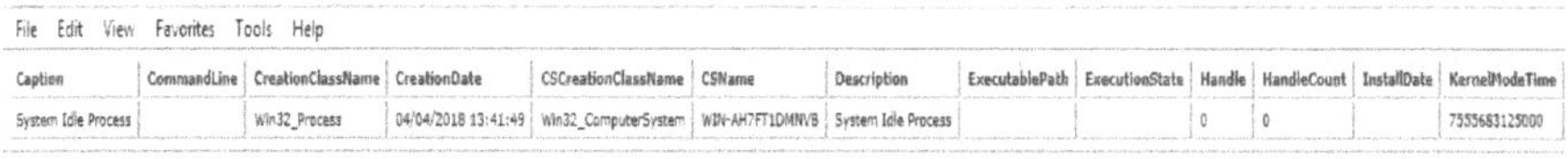

File Edit View Favorites Tools Help

Caption	CommandLine	CreationClassName	CreationDate	CSCreationClassName	CSName	Description	ExecutablePath	ExecutionState	Handle	HandleCount	InstallDate	KernelModeTime
System Idle Process		Win32_Process	04/04/2018 13:41:49	Win32_ComputerSystem	WIN-AH7FT1DMNVB	System Idle Process			0	0		7555683125000

Multi line Horizontal xsl

Here's the code:

```
$l = CreateObject("WbemScripting.SWbemLocator")
$svc = $l.ConnectServer(".", "root\cimv2")
$svc.Security_.AuthenticationLevel = 6
$svc.Security_.ImpersonationLevel = 3
$objs = $svc.InstancesOf("Win32_Process")


$ws = CreateObject("WScript.Shell")
$fso = CreateObject("Scripting.FileSystemObject")
$txtstream = $fso.OpenTextFile($ws.CurrentDirectory + "\Process.xsl", 2, true, -2)
$txtstream.WriteLine("<?xml version=" + chr(34) + "1.0" + chr(34) + " encoding="
+ chr(34) + "UTF-8" + chr(34) + "?>")
$txtstream.WriteLine("<xsl:stylesheet version=" + chr(34) + "1.0" + chr(34) + "
xmlns:xsl=" + chr(34) + "http://www.w3.org/1999/XSL/Transform" + chr(34) + ">")
$txtstream.WriteLine("</head>")
$txtstream.WriteLine("<body bgcolor=" + chr(34) + "#333333" + chr(34) + ">")
$txtstream.WriteLine("<table colspacing=" + chr(34) + "3" + chr(34) + "
colpadding=" + chr(34) + "3" + chr(34) + ">")
$obj = $objs.ItemIndex(0)
$txtstream.writeline("<tr>")
For Each $prop In $obj.Properties_
   $txtstream.writeline("<th align='left' nowrap='true'>" + $prop.Name + "</th>")
Next
```

```
$txtstream.writeline("</tr>")
$txtstream.writeline("<xsl:for-each Select=" + chr(34) + "data/win32_process" +
chr(34) + ">")
$txtstream.writeline("<tr>")
For Each $prop In $obj.Properties_
   $txtstream.writeline("<td align='left' nowrap='true'><xsl:value-of select=" +
chr(34) + $prop.Name + chr(34) + "/></td>")
Next
$txtstream.writeline("</tr>")
$txtstream.writeline("</xsl:for-each>")
$txtstream.WriteLine("</table>")
$txtstream.WriteLine("</body>")
$txtstream.WriteLine("</html>")
$txtstream.WriteLine("</xsl:template>")
$txtstream.WriteLine("</xsl:stylesheet>")
$txtstream.Close()
```

Here's what it looks like:

Caption	CommandLine
System Idle Process	
System	
smss.exe	
csrss.exe	
csrss.exe	
wininit.exe	wininit.exe
winlogon.exe	winlogon.exe
services.exe	
lsass.exe	C:\\Windows\\system32\\lsass.exe
svchost.exe	C:\\Windows\\system32\\svchost.exe -k DcomLaunch
svchost.exe	C:\\Windows\\system32\\svchost.exe -k RPCSS
dwm.exe	\dwm.exe\
NVDisplay.Container.exe	\C:\\Program Files\\NVIDIA Corporation\\Display.NvContainer\\NVDisplay.Container.exe\ -s NVDisplay.ContainerLocalSystem -f \C:\\ProgramData\\NVIDIA\\NVDisplay.ContainerLocalSystem.log\ -l 3 -d \C:\\Program Files\\NVIDIA Corpora
svchost.exe	C:\\Windows\\System32\\svchost.exe -k LocalServiceNetworkRestricted
svchost.exe	C:\\Windows\\system32\\svchost.exe -k netsvcs
svchost.exe	C:\\Windows\\system32\\svchost.exe -k LocalService
svchost.exe	C:\\Windows\\system32\\svchost.exe -k NetworkService
svchost.exe	C:\\Windows\\System32\\svchost.exe -k LocalSystemNetworkRestricted
svchost.exe	C:\\Windows\\system32\\svchost.exe -k LocalServiceNoNetwork
spoolsv.exe	C:\\Windows\\System32\\spoolsv.exe
NVDisplay.Container.exe	\C:\\Program Files\\NVIDIA Corporation\\Display.NvContainer\\NVDisplay.Container.exe\ -f \C:\\ProgramData\\NVIDIA\\DisplaySessionContainer%d.log\ -d \C:\\Program Files\\NVIDIA Corporation\\Display.NvContainer\\plugins\\Session\
armsvc.exe	\C:\\Program Files (x86)\\Common Files\\Adobe\\ARM\\1.0\\armsvc.exe\
svchost.exe	C:\\Windows\\system32\\svchost.exe -k apphost
OfficeClickToRun.exe	\C:\\Program Files\\Common Files\\Microsoft Shared\\ClickToRun\\OfficeClickToRun.exe\ /service
svchost.exe	C:\\Windows\\System32\\svchost.exe -k utcsvc
inetinfo.exe	C:\\Windows\\system32\\inetsrv\\inetinfo.exe
IpOverUsbSvc.exe	\C:\\Program Files (x86)\\Common Files\\Microsoft Shared\\Phone Tools\\CoreCon\\11.0\\bin\\IpOverUsbSvc.exe\
mqsvc.exe	C:\\Windows\\system32\\mqsvc.exe
sqlservr.exe	\c:\\Program Files\\Microsoft SQL Server\\MSSQL10.SQLEXPRESS\\MSSQL\\Binn\\sqlservr.exe\ -sSQLEXPRESS
SMSvcHost.exe	C:\\Windows\\Microsoft.NET\\Framework64\\v4.0.30319\\SMSvcHost.exe
nvcontainer.exe	\C:\\Program Files\\NVIDIA Corporation\\NvContainer\\nvcontainer.exe\ -s NvContainerLocalSystem -a -f \C:\\ProgramData\\NVIDIA\\NvContainerLocalSystem.log\ -l 3 -d \C:\\Program Files\\NVIDIA Corporation\\NvContainer\\plugins\\L
NvTelemetryContainer.exe	\C:\\Program Files (x86)\\NVIDIA Corporation\\NvTelemetry\\NvTelemetryContainer.exe\ -s NvTelemetryContainer -f \C:\\ProgramData\\NVIDIA\\NvTelemetryContainer.log\ -l 3 -d \C:\\Program Files (x86)\\NVIDIA Corporation\\NvTelem
sqlwriter.exe	\c:\\Program Files\\Microsoft SQL Server\\90\\Shared\\sqlwriter.exe\
svchost.exe	C:\\Windows\\system32\\svchost.exe -k imgsvc
TeamViewer_Service.exe	\C:\\Program Files (x86)\\TeamViewer\\TeamViewer_Service.exe\
svchost.exe	C:\\Windows\\system32\\svchost.exe -k iissvcs
wlms.exe	C:\\Windows\\system32\\wlms\\wlms.exe
mqtgsvc.exe	C:\\Windows\\system32\\mqtgsvc.exe
SMSvcHost.exe	\C:\\Windows\\Microsoft.NET\\Framework64\\v4.0.30319\\SMSvcHost.exe\ -NetMsmqActivator
vmms.exe	C:\\Windows\\system32\\vmms.exe

Single Line Vertical

Here's the Code:

```
$l = CreateObject("WbemScripting.SWbemLocator")
$svc = $l.ConnectServer(".", "root\cimv2")
$svc.Security_.AuthenticationLevel = 6
$svc.Security_.ImpersonationLevel = 3
$objs = $svc.InstancesOf("Win32_Process")
```

```
$ws = CreateObject("WScript.Shell")
$fso = CreateObject("Scripting.FileSystemObject")
$txtstream = $fso.OpenTextFile($ws.CurrentDirectory + "\Process.xsl", 2, true, -2)
$txtstream.WriteLine("<?xml version=" + chr(34) + "1.0" + chr(34) + " encoding="
+ chr(34) + "UTF-8" + chr(34) + "?>")
$txtstream.WriteLine("<xsl:stylesheet version=" + chr(34) + "1.0" + chr(34) + "
xmlns:xsl=" + chr(34) + "http://www.w3.org/1999/XSL/Transform" + chr(34) + ">")
$txtstream.WriteLine("<xsl:template match=" + chr(34) + "/" + chr(34) + ">")
$txtstream.WriteLine("<html>")
$txtstream.WriteLine("<head>")
$txtstream.WriteLine("<title>Products</title>")
$txtstream.WriteLine("</head>")
$txtstream.WriteLine("<body bgcolor=" + chr(34) + "#333333" + chr(34) + ">")
$txtstream.WriteLine("<table colspacing=" + chr(34) + "3" + chr(34) + "
colpadding=" + chr(34) + "3" + chr(34) + ">")
$obj = $objs.ItemIndex(0)
For Each $prop In $obj.Properties_
   $txtstream.writeline("<tr><th align='left' nowrap='true'>" + $prop.Name +
"</th><td align='left' nowrap='true'><xsl:value-of select=" + chr(34) +
"data/win32_process/" + $prop.Name + chr(34) + "/></td></tr>")
Next
$txtstream.WriteLine("</table>")
$txtstream.WriteLine("</body>")
$txtstream.WriteLine("</html>")
$txtstream.WriteLine("</xsl:template>")
$txtstream.WriteLine("</xsl:stylesheet>")
$txtstream.Close()
```

Here's the view:

Caption	System Idle Process
CommandLine	
CreationClassName	Win32_Process
CreationDate	04/04/2018 13:41:49
CSCreationClassName	Win32_ComputerSystem
CSName	WIN-AH7FT1DMNVB
Description	System Idle Process
ExecutablePath	
ExecutionState	
Handle	0
HandleCount	0
InstallDate	
KernelModeTime	7555683125000
MaximumWorkingSetSize	
MinimumWorkingSetSize	
Name	Win32_Process
OSCreationClassName	Win32_OperatingSystem
OSName	Microsoft Windows Server 2012 R2 Standard Evaluation|C:\\Windows|\\Device\\Harddisk0\\Partition4
OtherOperationCount	0
OtherTransferCount	0
PageFaults	1
PageFileUsage	0
ParentProcessId	0
PeakPageFileUsage	0
PeakVirtualSize	65536
PeakWorkingSetSize	4
Priority	0
PrivatePageCount	0
ProcessId	0
QuotaNonPagedPoolUsage	0
QuotaPagedPoolUsage	0

Multi Line Vertical View

Here's the code:

```
$l = CreateObject("WbemScripting.SWbemLocator")
$svc = $l.ConnectServer(".", "root\cimv2")
$svc.Security_.AuthenticationLevel = 6
$svc.Security_.ImpersonationLevel = 3
$objs = $svc.InstancesOf("Win32_Process")


$ws = CreateObject("WScript.Shell")
$fso = CreateObject("Scripting.FileSystemObject")
$txtstream = $fso.OpenTextFile($ws.CurrentDirectory + "\Process.xsl", 2, true, -2)
$txtstream.WriteLine("<?xml version=" + chr(34) + "1.0" + chr(34) + " encoding="
+ chr(34) + "UTF-8" + chr(34) + "?>")
$txtstream.WriteLine("<xsl:stylesheet version=" + chr(34) + "1.0" + chr(34) + "
xmlns:xsl=" + chr(34) + "http://www.w3.org/1999/XSL/Transform" + chr(34) + ">")
$txtstream.WriteLine("<xsl:template match=" + chr(34) + "/" + chr(34) + ">")
$txtstream.WriteLine("<html>")
$txtstream.WriteLine("<head>")
$txtstream.WriteLine("<title>Products</title>")
$txtstream.WriteLine("</head>")
$txtstream.WriteLine("<body bgcolor=" + chr(34) + "#333333" + chr(34) + ">")
$txtstream.WriteLine("<table colspacing=" + chr(34) + "3" + chr(34) + "
colpadding=" + chr(34) + "3" + chr(34) + ">")
$obj = $objs.ItemIndex(0)
For Each $prop In $obj.Properties_
   $txtstream.writeline("<tr><th align='left' nowrap='true'>" + $prop.Name +
"</th><xsl:for-each select=" + chr(34) + "data/win32_process" + chr(34) + "><td
align='left' nowrap='true'><xsl:value-of select=" + chr(34) + $prop.Name + chr(34)
+ "/></td></xsl:for-each></tr>")
Next
$txtstream.WriteLine("</table>")
```

```
$txtstream.WriteLine("</body>")
$txtstream.WriteLine("</html>")
$txtstream.WriteLine("</xsl:template>")
$txtstream.WriteLine("</xsl:stylesheet>")
$txtstream.Close()
```

Here’s the visual results:

Caption	System Idle Process	System
CommandLine		
CreationClassName	Win32_Process	Win32_Process
CreationDate	04/04/2018 13:41:49	04/04/2018 13:41:49
CSCreationClassName	Win32_ComputerSystem	Win32_ComputerSystem
CSName	WIN-AH7FT1DMNVB	WIN-AH7FT1DMNVB
Description	System Idle Process	System
ExecutablePath		
ExecutionState		
Handle	0	4
HandleCount	0	894
InstallDate		
KernelModeTime	7555683125000	12400312500
MaximumWorkingSetSize		
MinimumWorkingSetSize		
Name	Win32_Process	Win32_Process
OSCreationClassName	Win32_OperatingSystem	Win32_OperatingSystem
OSName	Microsoft Windows Server 2012 R2 Standard Evaluation|C:\\Windows|\\Device\\Harddisk0\\Partition4	Microsoft Windows Server 2012 R2 Standard Evaluation|C
OtherOperationCount	0	13106
OtherTransferCount	0	303382
PageFaults	1	12509
PageFileUsage	0	108
ParentProcessId	0	0
PeakPageFileUsage	0	2060
PeakVirtualSize	65536	20660224
PeakWorkingSetSize	4	17064
Priority	0	8
PrivatePageCount	0	110592
ProcessId	0	0
QuotaNonPagedPoolUsage	0	0

Time to do some summary stuff

If you have gotten down to here you should be congratulating yourself for sticking with it. But this is just the beginning of your journey. We've covered a lot of moving parts so to speak. And I'm pretty sure that your wondering why this e-book stops here.

That's because as you will soon find out, another e-book is in the wings and it will be entirely based on code. That's right. All the code you ever wanted to see in on e-book.

Well, it is coming!

The question is, will you be ready for it?

Enjoy the rest of your life and welcome, once again to the world of Kixtart.

Appendix A

The getvalue routine

Instead of writing this a million times, here's the routine:

```
function GetValue($Name, $obj)

  $tempstr = $obj.GetObjectText_;
  $pname = $Name + " = "
  $pos = InStr($tempstr, $pname)
  If($pos > 0)
     $pos = $pos + Len($pname)
     $l = Len($tempstr)
     $l = $l - $pos
     $tempstr = SUBSTR($tempstr, $pos, $l)
     $p = instr($tempstr, ";")
     $tempstr = SUBSTR($tempstr, 1, $p-1)
     $tempstr = REPLACE($tempstr,"{", "")
     $tempstr = REPLACE($tempstr,"}", "")
     $tempstr = REPLACE($tempstr,chr(34), "")
     if($obj.Properties_.Item($Name).CIMType = 101)
  if(Len($tempstr) > 12)
   $tempstr = substr($tempstr, 5,2) + "/" + substr($tempstr, 7,2) + "/" +
substr($tempstr, 1,4) + " " + substr($tempstr, 9,2) + ":" + substr($tempstr, 11,2) +
":" + substr($tempstr, 13,2)
  EndIf
     EndIf
     $GetValue = $tempstr
  Else
```

```
    $GetValue = ""
  EndIf

EndFunction
```

Appendix B

The stylesheets

I created some stylesheets that I like. You may not. Either way, they are here just in case you want to use them.

None

```
$txtstream.WriteLine("th")
$txtstream.WriteLine("{")
$txtstream.WriteLine("COLOR: white;")
$txtstream.WriteLine("text-align: left;")
$txtstream.WriteLine("FONT-FAMILY: font-family:Cambria, serif;")
$txtstream.WriteLine("FONT-SIZE: 10px;")
$txtstream.WriteLine("background: linear-gradient(-135, navy, blue);")
$txtstream.WriteLine("}")
$txtstream.WriteLine("td")
$txtstream.WriteLine("{")
$txtstream.WriteLine("COLOR: white;")
$txtstream.WriteLine("text-align: left;")
$txtstream.WriteLine("FONT-FAMILY: font-family:Cambria, serif;")
$txtstream.WriteLine("FONT-SIZE: 12px;")
$txtstream.WriteLine("}")
$txtstream.WriteLine("</style>")
```

Black and White Text

```
$txtstream.WriteLine("th")
$txtstream.WriteLine("{")
$txtstream.WriteLine("COLOR: white;")
$txtstream.WriteLine("BACKGROUND-COLOR: black;")
$txtstream.WriteLine("FONT-FAMILY:font-family:Cambria, serif;")
$txtstream.WriteLine("FONT-SIZE: 12px;")
$txtstream.WriteLine("text-align: left;")
$txtstream.WriteLine("white-Space: nowrap;")
$txtstream.WriteLine("background: linear-gradient(-135, navy, blue);")
$txtstream.WriteLine("}")
$txtstream.WriteLine("td")
$txtstream.WriteLine("{")
$txtstream.WriteLine("COLOR: white;")
$txtstream.WriteLine("BACKGROUND-COLOR: black;")
$txtstream.WriteLine("FONT-FAMILY: font-family:Cambria, serif;")
$txtstream.WriteLine("FONT-SIZE: 12px;")
$txtstream.WriteLine("text-align: left;")
$txtstream.WriteLine("white-Space: nowrap;")
$txtstream.WriteLine("}")
$txtstream.WriteLine("div")
$txtstream.WriteLine("{")
$txtstream.WriteLine("COLOR: white;")
$txtstream.WriteLine("BACKGROUND-COLOR: black;")
$txtstream.WriteLine("FONT-FAMILY: font-family:Cambria, serif;")
$txtstream.WriteLine("FONT-SIZE: 10px;")
$txtstream.WriteLine("text-align: left;")
$txtstream.WriteLine("white-Space: nowrap;")
$txtstream.WriteLine("}")
$txtstream.WriteLine("span")
$txtstream.WriteLine("{")
$txtstream.WriteLine("COLOR: white;")
$txtstream.WriteLine("BACKGROUND-COLOR: black;")
$txtstream.WriteLine("FONT-FAMILY: font-family:Cambria, serif;")
$txtstream.WriteLine("FONT-SIZE: 10px;")
$txtstream.WriteLine("text-align: left;")
$txtstream.WriteLine("white-Space: nowrap;")
$txtstream.WriteLine("display:inline-block;")
$txtstream.WriteLine("width: 100%;")
$txtstream.WriteLine("}")
$txtstream.WriteLine("textarea")
```

```
$txtstream.WriteLine("{")
$txtstream.WriteLine("COLOR: white;")
$txtstream.WriteLine("BACKGROUND-COLOR: black;")
$txtstream.WriteLine("FONT-FAMILY: font-family:Cambria, serif;")
$txtstream.WriteLine("FONT-SIZE: 10px;")
$txtstream.WriteLine("text-align: left;")
$txtstream.WriteLine("white-Space: nowrap;")
$txtstream.WriteLine("width: 100%;")
$txtstream.WriteLine("}")
$txtstream.WriteLine("select")
$txtstream.WriteLine("{")
$txtstream.WriteLine("COLOR: white;")
$txtstream.WriteLine("BACKGROUND-COLOR: black;")
$txtstream.WriteLine("FONT-FAMILY: font-family:Cambria, serif;")
$txtstream.WriteLine("FONT-SIZE: 10px;")
$txtstream.WriteLine("text-align: left;")
$txtstream.WriteLine("white-Space: nowrap;")
$txtstream.WriteLine("width: 100%;")
$txtstream.WriteLine("}")
$txtstream.WriteLine("input")
$txtstream.WriteLine("{")
$txtstream.WriteLine("COLOR: white;")
$txtstream.WriteLine("BACKGROUND-COLOR: black;")
$txtstream.WriteLine("FONT-FAMILY: font-family:Cambria, serif;")
$txtstream.WriteLine("FONT-SIZE: 12px;")
$txtstream.WriteLine("text-align: left;")
$txtstream.WriteLine("display:table-cell;")
$txtstream.WriteLine("white-Space: nowrap;")
$txtstream.WriteLine("}")
$txtstream.WriteLine("h1 {")
$txtstream.WriteLine("color: antiquewhite;")
$txtstream.WriteLine("text-shadow: 1px 1px 1px black;")
$txtstream.WriteLine("padding: 3px;")
$txtstream.WriteLine("text-align: center;")
$txtstream.WriteLine("box-shadow: inset 2px 2px 5px rgba(0,0,0,0.5), inset -2px -
2px 5px rgba(255,255,255,0.5);")
$txtstream.WriteLine("}")
$txtstream.WriteLine("</style>")
```

Colored Text

```
$txtstream.WriteLine("th")
$txtstream.WriteLine("{")
$txtstream.WriteLine("COLOR: darkred;")
$txtstream.WriteLine("BACKGROUND-COLOR: #eeeeee;")
$txtstream.WriteLine("FONT-FAMILY:font-family:Cambria, serif;")
$txtstream.WriteLine("FONT-SIZE: 12px;")
$txtstream.WriteLine("text-align: left;")
$txtstream.WriteLine("white-Space: nowrap;")
$txtstream.WriteLine("background: linear-gradient(-135, navy, blue);")
$txtstream.WriteLine("}")
$txtstream.WriteLine("td")
$txtstream.WriteLine("{")
$txtstream.WriteLine("COLOR: navy;")
$txtstream.WriteLine("BACKGROUND-COLOR: #eeeeee;")
$txtstream.WriteLine("FONT-FAMILY: font-family:Cambria, serif;")
$txtstream.WriteLine("FONT-SIZE: 12px;")
$txtstream.WriteLine("text-align: left;")
$txtstream.WriteLine("white-Space: nowrap;")
$txtstream.WriteLine("}")
$txtstream.WriteLine("div")
$txtstream.WriteLine("{")
$txtstream.WriteLine("COLOR: white;")
$txtstream.WriteLine("BACKGROUND-COLOR: navy;")
$txtstream.WriteLine("FONT-FAMILY: font-family:Cambria, serif;")
$txtstream.WriteLine("FONT-SIZE: 10px;")
$txtstream.WriteLine("text-align: left;")
$txtstream.WriteLine("white-Space: nowrap;")
$txtstream.WriteLine("}")
$txtstream.WriteLine("span")
$txtstream.WriteLine("{")
$txtstream.WriteLine("COLOR: white;")
$txtstream.WriteLine("BACKGROUND-COLOR: navy;")
$txtstream.WriteLine("FONT-FAMILY: font-family:Cambria, serif;")
$txtstream.WriteLine("FONT-SIZE: 10px;")
$txtstream.WriteLine("text-align: left;")
$txtstream.WriteLine("white-Space: nowrap;")
$txtstream.WriteLine("display:inline-block;")
$txtstream.WriteLine("width: 100%;")
$txtstream.WriteLine("}")
```

```
$txtstream.WriteLine("textarea")
$txtstream.WriteLine("{")
$txtstream.WriteLine("COLOR: white;")
$txtstream.WriteLine("BACKGROUND-COLOR: navy;")
$txtstream.WriteLine("FONT-FAMILY: font-family:Cambria, serif;")
$txtstream.WriteLine("FONT-SIZE: 10px;")
$txtstream.WriteLine("text-align: left;")
$txtstream.WriteLine("white-Space: nowrap;")
$txtstream.WriteLine("width: 100%;")
$txtstream.WriteLine("}")
$txtstream.WriteLine("select")
$txtstream.WriteLine("{")
$txtstream.WriteLine("COLOR: white;")
$txtstream.WriteLine("BACKGROUND-COLOR: navy;")
$txtstream.WriteLine("FONT-FAMILY: font-family:Cambria, serif;")
$txtstream.WriteLine("FONT-SIZE: 10px;")
$txtstream.WriteLine("text-align: left;")
$txtstream.WriteLine("white-Space: nowrap;")
$txtstream.WriteLine("width: 100%;")
$txtstream.WriteLine("}")
$txtstream.WriteLine("input")
$txtstream.WriteLine("{")
$txtstream.WriteLine("COLOR: white;")
$txtstream.WriteLine("BACKGROUND-COLOR: navy;")
$txtstream.WriteLine("FONT-FAMILY: font-family:Cambria, serif;")
$txtstream.WriteLine("FONT-SIZE: 12px;")
$txtstream.WriteLine("text-align: left;")
$txtstream.WriteLine("display:table-cell;")
$txtstream.WriteLine("white-Space: nowrap;")
$txtstream.WriteLine("}")
$txtstream.WriteLine("h1 {")
$txtstream.WriteLine("color: antiquewhite;")
$txtstream.WriteLine("text-shadow: 1px 1px 1px black;")
$txtstream.WriteLine("padding: 3px;")
$txtstream.WriteLine("text-align: center;")
$txtstream.WriteLine("box-shadow: inset 2px 2px 5px rgba(0,0,0,0.5), inset -2px -
2px 5px rgba(255,255,255,0.5);")
$txtstream.WriteLine("}")
$txtstream.WriteLine("</style>")
```

```
$txtstream.WriteLine("th")
$txtstream.WriteLine("{")
$txtstream.WriteLine("COLOR: black;")
$txtstream.WriteLine("BACKGROUND-COLOR: white;")
$txtstream.WriteLine("FONT-FAMILY:font-family:Cambria, serif;")
$txtstream.WriteLine("FONT-SIZE: 12px;")
$txtstream.WriteLine("text-align: left;")
$txtstream.WriteLine("white-Space: nowrap;")
$txtstream.WriteLine("background: linear-gradient(-135, navy, blue);")
$txtstream.WriteLine("}")
$txtstream.WriteLine("td")
$txtstream.WriteLine("{")
$txtstream.WriteLine("COLOR: black;")
$txtstream.WriteLine("BACKGROUND-COLOR: white;")
$txtstream.WriteLine("FONT-FAMILY: font-family:Cambria, serif;")
$txtstream.WriteLine("FONT-SIZE: 12px;")
$txtstream.WriteLine("text-align: left;")
$txtstream.WriteLine("white-Space: nowrap;")
$txtstream.WriteLine("}")
$txtstream.WriteLine("div")
$txtstream.WriteLine("{")
$txtstream.WriteLine("COLOR: black;")
$txtstream.WriteLine("BACKGROUND-COLOR: white;")
$txtstream.WriteLine("FONT-FAMILY: font-family:Cambria, serif;")
$txtstream.WriteLine("FONT-SIZE: 10px;")
$txtstream.WriteLine("text-align: left;")
$txtstream.WriteLine("white-Space: nowrap;")
$txtstream.WriteLine("}")
$txtstream.WriteLine("span")
$txtstream.WriteLine("{")
$txtstream.WriteLine("COLOR: black;")
$txtstream.WriteLine("BACKGROUND-COLOR: white;")
$txtstream.WriteLine("FONT-FAMILY: font-family:Cambria, serif;")
$txtstream.WriteLine("FONT-SIZE: 10px;")
$txtstream.WriteLine("text-align: left;")
$txtstream.WriteLine("white-Space: nowrap;")
```

```
$txtstream.WriteLine("display:inline-block;")
$txtstream.WriteLine("width: 100%;")
$txtstream.WriteLine("}")
$txtstream.WriteLine("textarea")
$txtstream.WriteLine("{")
$txtstream.WriteLine("COLOR: black;")
$txtstream.WriteLine("BACKGROUND-COLOR: white;")
$txtstream.WriteLine("FONT-FAMILY: font-family:Cambria, serif;")
$txtstream.WriteLine("FONT-SIZE: 10px;")
$txtstream.WriteLine("text-align: left;")
$txtstream.WriteLine("white-Space: nowrap;")
$txtstream.WriteLine("width: 100%;")
$txtstream.WriteLine("}")
$txtstream.WriteLine("select")
$txtstream.WriteLine("{")
$txtstream.WriteLine("COLOR: black;")
$txtstream.WriteLine("BACKGROUND-COLOR: white;")
$txtstream.WriteLine("FONT-FAMILY: font-family:Cambria, serif;")
$txtstream.WriteLine("FONT-SIZE: 10px;")
$txtstream.WriteLine("text-align: left;")
$txtstream.WriteLine("white-Space: nowrap;")
$txtstream.WriteLine("width: 100%;")
$txtstream.WriteLine("}")
$txtstream.WriteLine("input")
$txtstream.WriteLine("{")
$txtstream.WriteLine("COLOR: black;")
$txtstream.WriteLine("BACKGROUND-COLOR: white;")
$txtstream.WriteLine("FONT-FAMILY: font-family:Cambria, serif;")
$txtstream.WriteLine("FONT-SIZE: 12px;")
$txtstream.WriteLine("text-align: left;")
$txtstream.WriteLine("display:table-cell;")
$txtstream.WriteLine("white-Space: nowrap;")
$txtstream.WriteLine("}")
$txtstream.WriteLine("h1 {")
$txtstream.WriteLine("color: antiquewhite;")
$txtstream.WriteLine("text-shadow: 1px 1px 1px black;")
$txtstream.WriteLine("padding: 3px;")
$txtstream.WriteLine("text-align: center;")
$txtstream.WriteLine("box-shadow: inset 2px 2px 5px rgba(0,0,0,0.5), inset -2px -
2px 5px rgba(255,255,255,0.5);")
```

```
$txtstream.WriteLine("}")
$txtstream.WriteLine("</style>")
```

3d

```
$txtstream.WriteLine("body")
$txtstream.WriteLine("{")
$txtstream.WriteLine("PADDING-RIGHT: 0px;")
$txtstream.WriteLine("PADDING-LEFT: 0px;")
$txtstream.WriteLine("PADDING-BOTTOM: 0px;")
$txtstream.WriteLine("MARGIN: 0px;")
$txtstream.WriteLine("COLOR: #333;")
$txtstream.WriteLine("PADDING-TOP: 0px;")
$txtstream.WriteLine("FONT-FAMILY: verdana, arial, helvetica, sans-serif;")
$txtstream.WriteLine("}")
$txtstream.WriteLine("table")
$txtstream.WriteLine("{")
$txtstream.WriteLine("BORDER-RIGHT: #999999 3px solid;")
$txtstream.WriteLine("PADDING-RIGHT: 6px;")
$txtstream.WriteLine("PADDING-LEFT: 6px;")
$txtstream.WriteLine("FONT-WEIGHT: Bold;")
$txtstream.WriteLine("FONT-SIZE: 14px;")
$txtstream.WriteLine("PADDING-BOTTOM: 6px;")
$txtstream.WriteLine("COLOR: Peru;")
$txtstream.WriteLine("LINE-HEIGHT: 14px;")
$txtstream.WriteLine("PADDING-TOP: 6px;")
$txtstream.WriteLine("BORDER-BOTTOM: #999 1px solid;")
$txtstream.WriteLine("BACKGROUND-COLOR: #eeeeee;")
$txtstream.WriteLine("FONT-FAMILY: verdana, arial, helvetica, sans-serif;")
$txtstream.WriteLine("FONT-SIZE: 12px;")
$txtstream.WriteLine("}")
$txtstream.WriteLine("th")
$txtstream.WriteLine("{")
$txtstream.WriteLine("BORDER-RIGHT: #999999 3px solid;")
$txtstream.WriteLine("PADDING-RIGHT: 6px;")
$txtstream.WriteLine("PADDING-LEFT: 6px;")
$txtstream.WriteLine("FONT-WEIGHT: Bold;")
$txtstream.WriteLine("FONT-SIZE: 14px;")
$txtstream.WriteLine("PADDING-BOTTOM: 6px;")
$txtstream.WriteLine("COLOR: darkred;")
```

```
$txtstream.WriteLine("LINE-HEIGHT: 14px;")
$txtstream.WriteLine("PADDING-TOP: 6px;")
$txtstream.WriteLine("BORDER-BOTTOM: #999 1px solid;")
$txtstream.WriteLine("BACKGROUND-COLOR: #eeeeee;")
$txtstream.WriteLine("FONT-FAMILY:font-family:Cambria, serif;")
$txtstream.WriteLine("FONT-SIZE: 12px;")
$txtstream.WriteLine("text-align: left;")
$txtstream.WriteLine("white-Space: nowrap;")
$txtstream.WriteLine("background: linear-gradient(-135, navy, blue);")
$txtstream.WriteLine("}")
$txtstream.WriteLine(".th")
$txtstream.WriteLine("{")
$txtstream.WriteLine("BORDER-RIGHT: #999999 2px solid;")
$txtstream.WriteLine("PADDING-RIGHT: 6px;")
$txtstream.WriteLine("PADDING-LEFT: 6px;")
$txtstream.WriteLine("FONT-WEIGHT: Bold;")
$txtstream.WriteLine("PADDING-BOTTOM: 6px;")
$txtstream.WriteLine("COLOR: black;")
$txtstream.WriteLine("PADDING-TOP: 6px;")
$txtstream.WriteLine("BORDER-BOTTOM: #999 2px solid;")
$txtstream.WriteLine("BACKGROUND-COLOR: #eeeeee;")
$txtstream.WriteLine("FONT-FAMILY: font-family:Cambria, serif;")
$txtstream.WriteLine("FONT-SIZE: 10px;")
$txtstream.WriteLine("text-align: right;")
$txtstream.WriteLine("white-Space: nowrap;")
$txtstream.WriteLine("}")
$txtstream.WriteLine("td")
$txtstream.WriteLine("{")
$txtstream.WriteLine("BORDER-RIGHT: #999999 3px solid;")
$txtstream.WriteLine("PADDING-RIGHT: 6px;")
$txtstream.WriteLine("PADDING-LEFT: 6px;")
$txtstream.WriteLine("FONT-WEIGHT: Normal;")
$txtstream.WriteLine("PADDING-BOTTOM: 6px;")
$txtstream.WriteLine("COLOR: navy;")
$txtstream.WriteLine("LINE-HEIGHT: 14px;")
$txtstream.WriteLine("PADDING-TOP: 6px;")
$txtstream.WriteLine("BORDER-BOTTOM: #999 1px solid;")
$txtstream.WriteLine("BACKGROUND-COLOR: #eeeeee;")
$txtstream.WriteLine("FONT-FAMILY: font-family:Cambria, serif;")
$txtstream.WriteLine("FONT-SIZE: 12px;")
```

```
$txtstream.WriteLine("text-align: left;")
$txtstream.WriteLine("white-Space: nowrap;")
$txtstream.WriteLine("}")
$txtstream.WriteLine("div")
$txtstream.WriteLine("{")
$txtstream.WriteLine("BORDER-RIGHT: #999999 3px solid;")
$txtstream.WriteLine("PADDING-RIGHT: 6px;")
$txtstream.WriteLine("PADDING-LEFT: 6px;")
$txtstream.WriteLine("FONT-WEIGHT: Normal;")
$txtstream.WriteLine("PADDING-BOTTOM: 6px;")
$txtstream.WriteLine("COLOR: white;")
$txtstream.WriteLine("PADDING-TOP: 6px;")
$txtstream.WriteLine("BORDER-BOTTOM: #999 1px solid;")
$txtstream.WriteLine("BACKGROUND-COLOR: navy;")
$txtstream.WriteLine("FONT-FAMILY: font-family:Cambria, serif;")
$txtstream.WriteLine("FONT-SIZE: 10px;")
$txtstream.WriteLine("text-align: left;")
$txtstream.WriteLine("white-Space: nowrap;")
$txtstream.WriteLine("}")
$txtstream.WriteLine("span")
$txtstream.WriteLine("{")
$txtstream.WriteLine("BORDER-RIGHT: #999999 3px solid;")
$txtstream.WriteLine("PADDING-RIGHT: 3px;")
$txtstream.WriteLine("PADDING-LEFT: 3px;")
$txtstream.WriteLine("FONT-WEIGHT: Normal;")
$txtstream.WriteLine("PADDING-BOTTOM: 3px;")
$txtstream.WriteLine("COLOR: white;")
$txtstream.WriteLine("PADDING-TOP: 3px;")
$txtstream.WriteLine("BORDER-BOTTOM: #999 1px solid;")
$txtstream.WriteLine("BACKGROUND-COLOR: navy;")
$txtstream.WriteLine("FONT-FAMILY: font-family:Cambria, serif;")
$txtstream.WriteLine("FONT-SIZE: 10px;")
$txtstream.WriteLine("text-align: left;")
$txtstream.WriteLine("white-Space: nowrap;")
$txtstream.WriteLine("display:inline-block;")
$txtstream.WriteLine("width: 100%;")
$txtstream.WriteLine("}")
$txtstream.WriteLine("textarea")
$txtstream.WriteLine("{")
$txtstream.WriteLine("BORDER-RIGHT: #999999 3px solid;")
```

```
$txtstream.WriteLine("PADDING-RIGHT: 3px;")
$txtstream.WriteLine("PADDING-LEFT: 3px;")
$txtstream.WriteLine("FONT-WEIGHT: Normal;")
$txtstream.WriteLine("PADDING-BOTTOM: 3px;")
$txtstream.WriteLine("COLOR: white;")
$txtstream.WriteLine("PADDING-TOP: 3px;")
$txtstream.WriteLine("BORDER-BOTTOM: #999 1px solid;")
$txtstream.WriteLine("BACKGROUND-COLOR: navy;")
$txtstream.WriteLine("FONT-FAMILY: font-family:Cambria, serif;")
$txtstream.WriteLine("FONT-SIZE: 10px;")
$txtstream.WriteLine("text-align: left;")
$txtstream.WriteLine("white-Space: nowrap;")
$txtstream.WriteLine("width: 100%;")
$txtstream.WriteLine("}")
$txtstream.WriteLine("select")
$txtstream.WriteLine("{")
$txtstream.WriteLine("BORDER-RIGHT: #999999 3px solid;")
$txtstream.WriteLine("PADDING-RIGHT: 6px;")
$txtstream.WriteLine("PADDING-LEFT: 6px;")
$txtstream.WriteLine("FONT-WEIGHT: Normal;")
$txtstream.WriteLine("PADDING-BOTTOM: 6px;")
$txtstream.WriteLine("COLOR: white;")
$txtstream.WriteLine("PADDING-TOP: 6px;")
$txtstream.WriteLine("BORDER-BOTTOM: #999 1px solid;")
$txtstream.WriteLine("BACKGROUND-COLOR: navy;")
$txtstream.WriteLine("FONT-FAMILY: font-family:Cambria, serif;")
$txtstream.WriteLine("FONT-SIZE: 10px;")
$txtstream.WriteLine("text-align: left;")
$txtstream.WriteLine("white-Space: nowrap;")
$txtstream.WriteLine("width: 100%;")
$txtstream.WriteLine("}")
$txtstream.WriteLine("input")
$txtstream.WriteLine("{")
$txtstream.WriteLine("BORDER-RIGHT: #999999 3px solid;")
$txtstream.WriteLine("PADDING-RIGHT: 3px;")
$txtstream.WriteLine("PADDING-LEFT: 3px;")
$txtstream.WriteLine("FONT-WEIGHT: Bold;")
$txtstream.WriteLine("PADDING-BOTTOM: 3px;")
$txtstream.WriteLine("COLOR: white;")
$txtstream.WriteLine("PADDING-TOP: 3px;")
```

```
$txtstream.WriteLine("BORDER-BOTTOM: #999 1px solid;")
$txtstream.WriteLine("BACKGROUND-COLOR: navy;")
$txtstream.WriteLine("FONT-FAMILY: font-family:Cambria, serif;")
$txtstream.WriteLine("FONT-SIZE: 12px;")
$txtstream.WriteLine("text-align: left;")
$txtstream.WriteLine("display:table-cell;")
$txtstream.WriteLine("white-Space: nowrap;")
$txtstream.WriteLine("width: 100%;")
$txtstream.WriteLine("}")
$txtstream.WriteLine("h1 {")
$txtstream.WriteLine("color: antiquewhite;")
$txtstream.WriteLine("text-shadow: 1px 1px 1px black;")
$txtstream.WriteLine("padding: 3px;")
$txtstream.WriteLine("text-align: center;")
$txtstream.WriteLine("box-shadow: inset 2px 2px 5px rgba(0,0,0,0.5), inset -2px -
2px 5px rgba(255,255,255,0.5);")
$txtstream.WriteLine("}")
$txtstream.WriteLine("</style>")
```

Shadow Box

```
$txtstream.WriteLine("body")
$txtstream.WriteLine("{")
$txtstream.WriteLine("PADDING-RIGHT: 0px;")
$txtstream.WriteLine("PADDING-LEFT: 0px;")
$txtstream.WriteLine("PADDING-BOTTOM: 0px;")
$txtstream.WriteLine("MARGIN: 0px;")
$txtstream.WriteLine("COLOR: #333;")
$txtstream.WriteLine("PADDING-TOP: 0px;")
$txtstream.WriteLine("FONT-FAMILY: verdana, arial, helvetica, sans-serif;")
$txtstream.WriteLine("}")
$txtstream.WriteLine(".myclass")
$txtstream.WriteLine("{")
$txtstream.WriteLine("BORDER-RIGHT: #999999 3px solid;")
$txtstream.WriteLine("PADDING-RIGHT: 6px;")
$txtstream.WriteLine("PADDING-LEFT: 6px;")
$txtstream.WriteLine("PADDING-BOTTOM: 6px;")
$txtstream.WriteLine("LINE-HEIGHT: 14px;")
$txtstream.WriteLine("PADDING-TOP: 6px;")
$txtstream.WriteLine("BORDER-BOTTOM: #999 1px solid;")
```

```
$txtstream.WriteLine("BACKGROUND-COLOR: #eeeeee;")
$txtstream.WriteLine("filter:progid:DXImageTransform.Microsoft.Shadow(color='w
hite', Direction=135, Strength=16)")
$txtstream.WriteLine("}")
$txtstream.WriteLine(".myclass1")
$txtstream.WriteLine("{")
$txtstream.WriteLine("BORDER-RIGHT: #999999 3px solid;")
$txtstream.WriteLine("PADDING-RIGHT: 6px;")
$txtstream.WriteLine("PADDING-LEFT: 6px;")
$txtstream.WriteLine("PADDING-BOTTOM: 6px;")
$txtstream.WriteLine("LINE-HEIGHT: 14px;")
$txtstream.WriteLine("PADDING-TOP: 6px;")
$txtstream.WriteLine("BORDER-BOTTOM: #999 1px solid;")
$txtstream.WriteLine("BACKGROUND-COLOR: #eeeeee;")
$txtstream.WriteLine("filter:progid:DXImageTransform.Microsoft.Shadow(color='sil
ver', Direction=135, Strength=16)")
$txtstream.WriteLine("}")
$txtstream.WriteLine("th")
$txtstream.WriteLine("{")
$txtstream.WriteLine("BORDER-RIGHT: #999999 3px solid;")
$txtstream.WriteLine("PADDING-RIGHT: 6px;")
$txtstream.WriteLine("PADDING-LEFT: 6px;")
$txtstream.WriteLine("FONT-WEIGHT: Bold;")
$txtstream.WriteLine("FONT-SIZE: 14px;")
$txtstream.WriteLine("PADDING-BOTTOM: 6px;")
$txtstream.WriteLine("COLOR: darkred;")
$txtstream.WriteLine("LINE-HEIGHT: 14px;")
$txtstream.WriteLine("PADDING-TOP: 6px;")
$txtstream.WriteLine("BORDER-BOTTOM: #999 1px solid;")
$txtstream.WriteLine("BACKGROUND-COLOR: #eeeeee;")
$txtstream.WriteLine("FONT-FAMILY:font-family:Cambria, serif;")
$txtstream.WriteLine("FONT-SIZE: 12px;")
$txtstream.WriteLine("text-align: left;")
$txtstream.WriteLine("white-Space: nowrap;")
$txtstream.WriteLine("background: linear-gradient(-135, #41361d, #6a4740);")
$txtstream.WriteLine("}")
$txtstream.WriteLine(".th")
$txtstream.WriteLine("{")
$txtstream.WriteLine("BORDER-RIGHT: #999999 2px solid;")
$txtstream.WriteLine("PADDING-RIGHT: 6px;")
```

```
$txtstream.WriteLine("PADDING-LEFT: 6px;")
$txtstream.WriteLine("FONT-WEIGHT: Bold;")
$txtstream.WriteLine("PADDING-BOTTOM: 6px;")
$txtstream.WriteLine("COLOR: black;")
$txtstream.WriteLine("PADDING-TOP: 6px;")
$txtstream.WriteLine("BORDER-BOTTOM: #999 2px solid;")
$txtstream.WriteLine("BACKGROUND-COLOR: #eeeeee;")
$txtstream.WriteLine("FONT-FAMILY: font-family:Cambria, serif;")
$txtstream.WriteLine("FONT-SIZE: 10px;")
$txtstream.WriteLine("text-align: right;")
$txtstream.WriteLine("white-Space: nowrap;")
$txtstream.WriteLine("}")
$txtstream.WriteLine("td")
$txtstream.WriteLine("{")
$txtstream.WriteLine("BORDER-RIGHT: #999999 3px solid;")
$txtstream.WriteLine("PADDING-RIGHT: 6px;")
$txtstream.WriteLine("PADDING-LEFT: 6px;")
$txtstream.WriteLine("FONT-WEIGHT: Normal;")
$txtstream.WriteLine("PADDING-BOTTOM: 6px;")
$txtstream.WriteLine("COLOR: navy;")
$txtstream.WriteLine("LINE-HEIGHT: 14px;")
$txtstream.WriteLine("PADDING-TOP: 6px;")
$txtstream.WriteLine("BORDER-BOTTOM: #999 1px solid;")
$txtstream.WriteLine("BACKGROUND-COLOR: #eeeeee;")
$txtstream.WriteLine("FONT-FAMILY: font-family:Cambria, serif;")
$txtstream.WriteLine("FONT-SIZE: 12px;")
$txtstream.WriteLine("text-align: left;")
$txtstream.WriteLine("white-Space: nowrap;")
$txtstream.WriteLine("}")
$txtstream.WriteLine("div")
$txtstream.WriteLine("{")
$txtstream.WriteLine("BORDER-RIGHT: #999999 3px solid;")
$txtstream.WriteLine("PADDING-RIGHT: 6px;")
$txtstream.WriteLine("PADDING-LEFT: 6px;")
$txtstream.WriteLine("FONT-WEIGHT: Normal;")
$txtstream.WriteLine("PADDING-BOTTOM: 6px;")
$txtstream.WriteLine("COLOR: white;")
$txtstream.WriteLine("PADDING-TOP: 6px;")
$txtstream.WriteLine("BORDER-BOTTOM: #999 1px solid;")
$txtstream.WriteLine("BACKGROUND-COLOR: navy;")
```

```
$txtstream.WriteLine("FONT-FAMILY: font-family:Cambria, serif;")
$txtstream.WriteLine("FONT-SIZE: 10px;")
$txtstream.WriteLine("text-align: left;")
$txtstream.WriteLine("white-Space: nowrap;")
$txtstream.WriteLine("}")
$txtstream.WriteLine("span")
$txtstream.WriteLine("{")
$txtstream.WriteLine("BORDER-RIGHT: #999999 3px solid;")
$txtstream.WriteLine("PADDING-RIGHT: 3px;")
$txtstream.WriteLine("PADDING-LEFT: 3px;")
$txtstream.WriteLine("FONT-WEIGHT: Normal;")
$txtstream.WriteLine("PADDING-BOTTOM: 3px;")
$txtstream.WriteLine("COLOR: white;")
$txtstream.WriteLine("PADDING-TOP: 3px;")
$txtstream.WriteLine("BORDER-BOTTOM: #999 1px solid;")
$txtstream.WriteLine("BACKGROUND-COLOR: navy;")
$txtstream.WriteLine("FONT-FAMILY: font-family:Cambria, serif;")
$txtstream.WriteLine("FONT-SIZE: 10px;")
$txtstream.WriteLine("text-align: left;")
$txtstream.WriteLine("white-Space: nowrap;")
$txtstream.WriteLine("display:inline-block;")
$txtstream.WriteLine("width: 100%;")
$txtstream.WriteLine("}")
$txtstream.WriteLine("textarea")
$txtstream.WriteLine("{")
$txtstream.WriteLine("BORDER-RIGHT: #999999 3px solid;")
$txtstream.WriteLine("PADDING-RIGHT: 3px;")
$txtstream.WriteLine("PADDING-LEFT: 3px;")
$txtstream.WriteLine("FONT-WEIGHT: Normal;")
$txtstream.WriteLine("PADDING-BOTTOM: 3px;")
$txtstream.WriteLine("COLOR: white;")
$txtstream.WriteLine("PADDING-TOP: 3px;")
$txtstream.WriteLine("BORDER-BOTTOM: #999 1px solid;")
$txtstream.WriteLine("BACKGROUND-COLOR: navy;")
$txtstream.WriteLine("FONT-FAMILY: font-family:Cambria, serif;")
$txtstream.WriteLine("FONT-SIZE: 10px;")
$txtstream.WriteLine("text-align: left;")
$txtstream.WriteLine("white-Space: nowrap;")
$txtstream.WriteLine("width: 100%;")
$txtstream.WriteLine("}")
```

```
$txtstream.WriteLine("select")
$txtstream.WriteLine("{")
$txtstream.WriteLine("BORDER-RIGHT: #999999 3px solid;")
$txtstream.WriteLine("PADDING-RIGHT: 6px;")
$txtstream.WriteLine("PADDING-LEFT: 6px;")
$txtstream.WriteLine("FONT-WEIGHT: Normal;")
$txtstream.WriteLine("PADDING-BOTTOM: 6px;")
$txtstream.WriteLine("COLOR: white;")
$txtstream.WriteLine("PADDING-TOP: 6px;")
$txtstream.WriteLine("BORDER-BOTTOM: #999 1px solid;")
$txtstream.WriteLine("BACKGROUND-COLOR: navy;")
$txtstream.WriteLine("FONT-FAMILY: font-family:Cambria, serif;")
$txtstream.WriteLine("FONT-SIZE: 10px;")
$txtstream.WriteLine("text-align: left;")
$txtstream.WriteLine("white-Space: nowrap;")
$txtstream.WriteLine("width: 100%;")
$txtstream.WriteLine("}")
$txtstream.WriteLine("input")
$txtstream.WriteLine("{")
$txtstream.WriteLine("BORDER-RIGHT: #999999 3px solid;")
$txtstream.WriteLine("PADDING-RIGHT: 3px;")
$txtstream.WriteLine("PADDING-LEFT: 3px;")
$txtstream.WriteLine("FONT-WEIGHT: Bold;")
$txtstream.WriteLine("PADDING-BOTTOM: 3px;")
$txtstream.WriteLine("COLOR: white;")
$txtstream.WriteLine("PADDING-TOP: 3px;")
$txtstream.WriteLine("BORDER-BOTTOM: #999 1px solid;")
$txtstream.WriteLine("BACKGROUND-COLOR: navy;")
$txtstream.WriteLine("FONT-FAMILY: font-family:Cambria, serif;")
$txtstream.WriteLine("FONT-SIZE: 12px;")
$txtstream.WriteLine("text-align: left;")
$txtstream.WriteLine("display:table-cell;")
$txtstream.WriteLine("white-Space: nowrap;")
$txtstream.WriteLine("width: 100%;")
$txtstream.WriteLine("}")
$txtstream.WriteLine("h1 {")
$txtstream.WriteLine("color: antiquewhite;")
$txtstream.WriteLine("text-shadow: 1px 1px 1px black;")
$txtstream.WriteLine("padding: 3px;")
$txtstream.WriteLine("text-align: center;")
```

```
$txtstream.WriteLine("box-shadow: inset 2px 2px 5px rgba(0,0,0,0.5), inset -2px -2px 5px rgba(255,255,255,0.5);")
$txtstream.WriteLine("}")
$txtstream.WriteLine("</style>")
```

www.ingramcontent.com/pod-product-compliance
Lightning Source LLC
Chambersburg PA
CBHW071549080326
40690CB00056B/1613

* 9 7 8 1 7 2 0 8 7 0 9 4 4 *